Jen Eskridge

Free-Motion Framework

10 Innovative Wholecloth Quilt Designs

8 Skill-Building Lessons

stash BOOKS®

an imprint of C&T Publishing

Text copyright © 2018 by Jen Eskridge

Photography and artwork copyright © 2018 by C&T Publishing, Inc.

Publisher: Amy Marson

Creative Director: Gailen Runge

Editors: Liz Aneloski and Katie Van Amburg

Technical Editor: Linda Johnson

Cover/Book Designer: April Mostek

Production Coordinator: Zinnia Heinzmann

Production Editor: Alice Mace Nakanishi

Illustrators: Valyrie Gillum and Kirstie L. Pettersen

Subjects photography by Lucy Glover and instructional photography
by Mail Yong Vang of C&T Publishing, Inc., unless otherwise noted

Published by Stash Books, an imprint of C&T Publishing, Inc., P.O. Box 1456,
Lafayette, CA 94549

Library of Congress Cataloging-in-Publication Data

Names: Eskridge, Jen (Jennifer Reanna), author.

Title: Free-motion framework : 10 innovative wholecloth quilt designs --
8 skill-building lessons / Jen Eskridge.

Description: Lafayette, CA : C&T Publishing, Inc., 2018.

Identifiers: LCCN 2017043059 | ISBN 9781617456060 (soft cover)

Subjects: LCSH: Machine quilting--Patterns. | Wholecloth quilts.

Classification: LCC TT835 .E833 2018 | DDC 746.46/041--dc23

LC record available at https://lccn.loc.gov/2017043059

Printed in China

10 9 8 7 6 5 4 3 2 1

Dedication

This book is dedicated to every person who has attended a quilt show and thought, "I wish I could do that." You are my inspiration, and this book is for you. Dream big!

Acknowledgments

Thank you to the fantastic companies who generously provided supplies and tools to make this book possible.

▸ Handi Quilter (handiquilter.com) provided the Handi VersaTool machine quilting ruler.

▸ Fairfield (fairfieldworld.com) provided batting for all the quilted projects in this book.

▸ Fil-Tec / Bobbin Central (bobbincentral.com) provided thread in every color of the rainbow.

▸ Clover USA (clover-usa.com) provided dressmaker's tracing paper and a tracing wheel, Wonder Clips, and water-soluble marking tools.

This book is an absolute passion of mine, but would not have come to fruition without help from some strangers. Okay, they aren't *that* strange; after all, they are quilters! I was lucky to work with 16 different machine quilters in this endeavor. Some I had met before, and others trusted me and jumped in with both feet. Without you all, this book wouldn't be possible.

A huge thank you to the quilting team:

Colleen Eskridge	Jo Oliver	Karlee Porter	Shannon Schlosser
Erin Monfort-Nelson	Joanna Marsh	Laura Pukstas	Sterling LaBosky
Geraldine A. Wilkins	Joey Strange	Marion McClellan	Susan Lawson
Helen Ernst	Karen Morello	Melanie Leckey	Teresa Silva

Many quilters listed above have quilting businesses. Please take the time to learn more about them in Contributing Quilters (page 126).

Lastly, thanks to my family. Thank you to the members of my immediate family, who don't seem to mind a longarm in the dining room and sandwiches for dinner. Thank you to my mother and my mother-in-law, both of whom are longarm quilters and don't mind me spending entire phone conversations rambling on about tension, echoing styles, and upcoming quilt shows. Thank you to my industrious father, who decided to learn how to disassemble, clean, maintain, and rebuild my sewing machines. Thank you to my husband who has always supported my sewing and quilting business. Y'all mean the world to me.

Contents

Section 1: Wholecloth Free-Motion Quilting   9

Quilting Skill Builder Process

· *Reflection*

· *Set goals*

· *Brainstorm ideas*

· *Print and mark design lines*

· *Transfer design lines to quilt*

· *Layer and quilt*

· *The unexpected results*

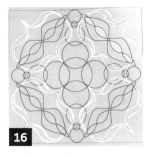

Isolating Shapes

· *Choosing marked lines*

· *How to use marked lines*

Quilting Ideas and Goals

· *Using rulers*

· *Quilting fills*

Quilting Goals Worksheet

Making Larger Quilts

· *Borders*

· *Multiples*

Simple Quilt Block Concepts

· *Use linear designs to finish traditional quilts*

Thread and Batting

· *Considerations when choosing threads*

· *Batting*

Blocking

· *How to block a quilt*

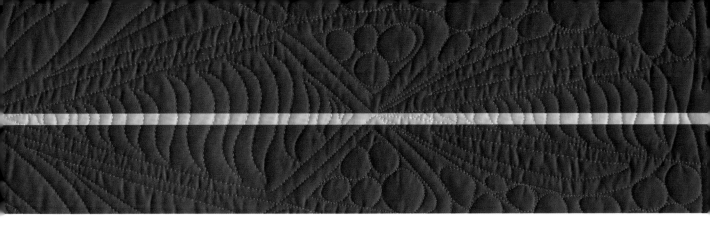

Section 2: The Quilts   65

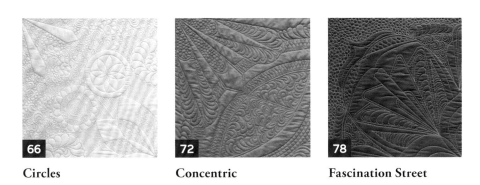

66

Circles

72

Concentric

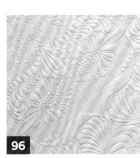

78

Fascination Street

84

Flora and Spike

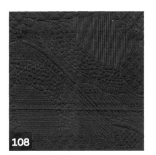

90

Ginkgo

96

Grammar Nut

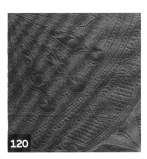

102

Shark Attack

108

Solar System

114

The Grid

120

The Pinch

Introduction

Wholecloth quilts are incredible pieces of folk art history. Over time, they have evolved to become masterful works of art of the highest skill level. If a wholecloth quilt is on display at any quilt show, I find myself staring at it with curiosity and wonder.

After seeing so many amazing wholecloth quilts, I started to ask myself questions: How could I make one? Where would I start? How could I break down the design elements and make these classic treasures accessible to regular quilters like me?

You know what they say: "Eat an elephant one bite at a time." That was the mantra and basic concept fueling my idea for *Free-Motion Framework*.

You might not initially have the skill level to design and quilt a jaw-dropping wholecloth quilt, but if you set forth on a journey to build your skills, you can create one—using my method for generating a wholecloth quilt, which excludes the elaborate and intimidating planning-every-stitch phase.

Preprinted wholecloth quilts are available to consumers. They are beautiful, but not very unique: When different quilters stitch on planned, marked stitching lines, their quilts end up looking very similar. Additionally, if you use someone else's wholecloth design, you don't have a choice in the skill level.

When you see the process and simplicity I'm proposing, I have no doubt that you will make a unique, interesting, and fantastic wholecloth quilt. I cannot wait to see it!

Keep in mind, the wholecloth is simply a by-product of your diligent skills practice. Each quilt in this book is designed purely as a quilting skill-builder exercise that happens to produce a wholecloth quilt. The projects finish about 40″ × 40″ square. I found that being able to finish a project helps increase your confidence and willingness to approach it. Diving into a king-size, traditional, white wholecloth may not offer the same success. By working in a smaller size, the pressure to make a perfect piece is lessened. Take your time, work in chunks of space, and try new things.

One bite at a time, friends!

Speaking of breaking tradition, you'll find that no white quilts are featured in this book. There are already many white wholecloth quilts. I wanted to take this opportunity to jazz up the concept with bright and vibrant tones.

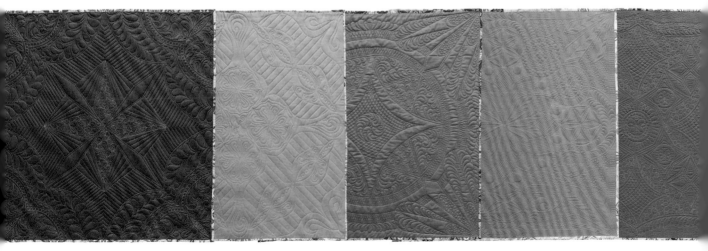

In This Book

Use this book as an easy step-by-step guide to practice machine quilting skills while producing a wholecloth wall-hanging or baby quilt; find directions to produce larger quilts in Making Larger Quilts (page 55). With a commitment to practice sketched ideas and goals, and only approximately 2½ yards of fabric, you'll see marked improvement in your quilting skills.

LINES FOR QUILTING

Linear concepts are presented in these ten designs: Circles (page 66), Concentric (page 72), Fascination Street (page 78), Flora and Spike (page 84), Ginkgo (page 90), Grammar Nut (page 96), Shark Attack (page 102), Solar System (page 108), The Grid (page 114), and The Pinch (page 120).

DOWNLOADING DESIGNS AND WORKSHEETS

Each linear design (in three size formats) and corresponding worksheet are available online as a downloadable PDF:

tinyurl.com/11283-patterns-download ◄ ·

The downloadable formats for each of the ten linear designs include (in this order):

▸ **A Quilting Goals Worksheet that corresponds with each design:**
  Each full-page worksheet prints on 8½″ × 11″ paper. For more about the worksheets, see Quilting Skill Builder Process (page 10) and Quilting Goals Worksheet (page 38).

▸ **A complete design in two sizes—12″ × 12″ and 15″ × 15″—to be used to quilt traditional quilt blocks:**
  Each design prints on four sheets of 8½″ × 11″ paper, which will need to be taped together.
  For more information about using these sizes, see Simple Quilt Block Concepts (page 57).

▸ **A full-size 20″ × 20″ quadrant of the design to be used to make the wholecloth skill builder quilt:**
  This full-size quadrant prints on six sheets of 8½″ × 11″ paper, which will need to be taped together.
  For more information, see Quilting Skill Builder Process (page 10).

▸ ***BONUS DOWNLOADS:* Three oversized pages of each design—the full-size 20″ × 20″ quadrant and the complete designs in 12″ × 12″ and 15″ × 15″ sizes:**
  Each of these pages may be printed at a copy shop on a single sheet of oversized paper (no taping required).

EXTRA OPTION

Here's an option with no downloading, no printing, no copying, and no taping …

Free-Motion Framework Full-Size Pattern Sheets *by Jen Eskridge (available from C&T Publishing).*

This packet contains 12 preprinted pattern sheets:

• *10 full-size 20″ × 20″ quadrants—one from each design in* Free-Motion Framework

• *Plus 2 brand-new complete designs—one for a 12″ × 12″ block and one for a 15″ × 15″ block*

Free-Motion Framework

1

Wholecloth Free-Motion Quilting

Quilting Skill Builder Process

STEP 1: REFLECTION

Even the most advanced quilters have design styles or areas that may benefit from a bit more practice. Reflection is the first step in assessing what your style may need and will help you set goals for yourself.

To start, ask yourself a few questions. For example:

▶ What designs would I like to improve?

▶ Is scale or density an area that needs attention?

▶ Can I increase my speed without compromising my design integrity?

There are many areas on which each individual quilter may choose to focus. While quite a few are outlined in this book, you can always add more to suit your own skill level, style, and design aesthetic.

Note: *It is important to remember this is a reflection step, not a free pass to be "your own worst critic." This is not a place for self-doubt. Your quilting is amazing, and you are taking it to the next level!*

STEP 2: SET GOALS

After reflection, iron out a few goals for yourself. Each design chapter includes a Quilting Goals Worksheet (page 39) for you to either copy or to download and print. (For download instructions, see Downloading Designs and Worksheets, page 7.) By taking the time to write your goals on the provided worksheet, you will have a better focus when quilting the skill builder projects.

If you are committed to working on improving sets of skills, it is extremely helpful to save your completed Quilting Goals Worksheets. Not only will you see how far you've progressed, but you'll have reference sheets for future design work.

Specific goals are addressed in depth in Quilting Ideas and Goals (page 22).

Quilting Goals Worksheet

Write goals here, such as "Feathers within a shape" or "Quarter Inch echoes."

Practice Sketches

STEP 3: BRAINSTORM IDEAS

What type of quilting styles will you choose to practice? The answers are limitless! It is interesting to note that the answers vary from person to person and change, develop, and evolve as you improve.

Ten unique linear designs are provided in this book. Each design section provides the opportunity to trace/stitch marked lines and fill in created outlined shapes. The beauty is that there is zero obligation to trace every single line and zero obligation to fill every shape. As you'll see, no two quilts look the same.

When you look at the linear designs, think in terms of small shapes to fill. Small shapes are easy to work with and complete. Quilting fill ideas can be found in Quilting Ideas and Goals (page 22).

Refer to the chapter Quilting Goals Worksheet (page 38) to help you plan your quilting designs.

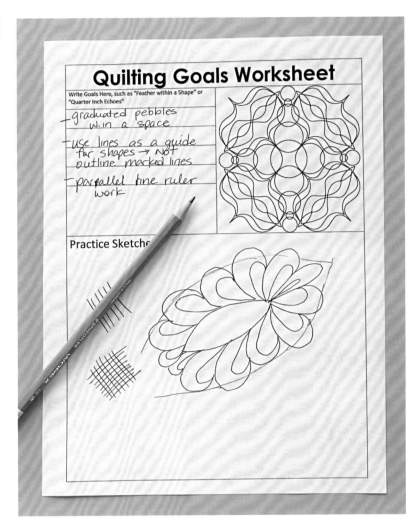

Quilting Goals Worksheet

Write Goals Here, such as "Feather within a Shape" or "Quarter Inch Echoes"

- graduated pebbles w. in a space
- use lines as a guide for shapes → Not outline marked lines
- parallel line ruler work

Practice Sketche

STEP 4: PRINT AND MARK DESIGN LINES

Choose one of the ten linear designs found in the beginning of each quilt chapter, following Section 2: The Quilts (page 65).

Note: *Don't be intimidated by the number of lines in the original design. Remember, you do* not *need to use them all.*

TIP If you are a planner, color in the linear design in the upper right corner of the Quilting Goals Worksheet. This helps identify shapes. You may want to use an assortment of colored pencils to shade shapes and assign the colors to a fill design. For more information on isolating shapes, see Isolating Shapes (page 16).

4. Prepare fabric by pressing a horizontal and vertical fold line to divide it into 4 equal parts.

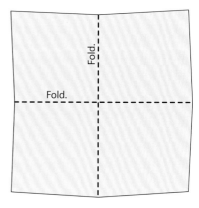

Note: If you prefer to avoid downloading, printing, and taping the design together, see Extra Option (page 7).

1. Download the 20″ × 20″ quadrant associated with the design of your choice (see Downloading the Designs, page 7).

2. To print, determine which are the 8½″ × 11″ tiled pages and fill in the Page Range. Press Print.

Note: There is a full-size option in the file that can be taken to a copy shop and printed out in one piece.

3. Use the design lines as reference marks to tape together the 6 pages.

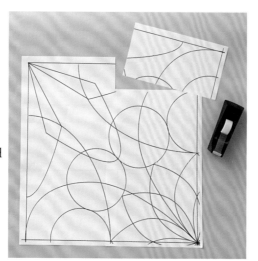

STEP 5: TRANSFER DESIGN LINES TO QUILT

1. Based on your workspace and materials, choose one of the following options to trace all lines onto the fabric with a water-soluble or non-permanent marking tool. (*Note:* Tracing the perimeter square is extremely helpful, too.)

▶ If the fabric is light enough, you may opt to lay the quadrant on a large work surface or table and simply trace the design lines though the fabric.

▶ Use dressmaker's marking tools (dressmaker's carbon/tracing paper and a tracing wheel). Test the carbon on the fabric to ensure it will wash out. On a large cutting mat, place the carbon (color side down) on top of the 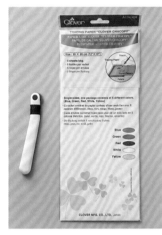 fabric and under the quadrant. Use the tracing wheel to go over and mark each line, moving the carbon as needed.

▶ Try tracing the design onto plastic wrap (such as Glad Press'n Seal) or lightweight tissue paper. Fix the traced design to the right side of the quilt top and sew right through the plastic or tissue.

▶ Use a lightboard or lightbox to transfer the desired lines to the quilt top. Tape the paper design in place on the lightboard and lay the quilt block over the design. Trace with a water-soluble pen or chalk.

▶ Don't have a lightboard? Using blue painter's tape, adhere the desired lines page to a large window and tape the quilt over the design.

▶ Don't have a large window or don't want to work vertically? Place a flashlight in a plastic storage bin. Purchase a Plexiglas sheet just large enough to cover the top of the storage bin. Tape the desired lines page to the Plexiglas and lay the quilt over the lines. Instant lightbox!

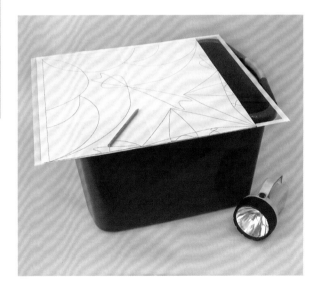

TIP If you have a large enough work surface, table, or window, you can eliminate the need to turn and align the design by printing four copies of the quadrant. Tape together all four to create a full-size design to trace.

Note: *In all designs, the horizontal and vertical centerlines are marked on each quadrant. For even more design options, consider using a different corner as the quadrant's center.*

2. Remove the fabric. Rotate it 90°, aligning the center again. Tape and trace as before.

3. Trace the remaining quadrants in this manner.

Note: *If the tracing is "off" or the center isn't perfect, you have two options:*

• *Using a ruler, manipulate the lines slightly to create a perfect intersection with perfect points in the desired area. Use a wet cotton swab to remove water-soluble lines that are askew.*

• *Leave the lines and treat the center as its own shape. Simply cover that area with a quilting fill; after all, you are the only one who will know where the lines were when the quilt is finished.*

STEP 6: LAYER AND QUILT

Prepare the quilt sandwich.

Longarm quilters: **If you opt to work from the center outward before beginning to quilt the actual design lines, it is useful to set the machine to a large basting stitch and baste the quilt.**

Working from the center, start by outlining a few marked lines. Don't feel pressured to outline the entire design. When you work in small chunks, the design will develop as it's quilted.

Shapes start to appear, rather than comprehensive design lines. Perfect! Isolate those shapes to start.

If you plan on quilting over a period of time, it is helpful to draw what you just quilted in fabric onto the paper template. This will be your reference as you finish each area of the quilt.

Note: *Working symmetrically creates the illusion that this wholecloth quilt was a masterfully planned concept, rather than a wildly interesting practice piece.*

If one of your goals is to echo quilting lines with accuracy, stitch the echoes ¹⁄₁₆″, ⅛″, or ¼″ from the marked lines.

With a few shapes stitched, and echoed if applicable, start to quilt within the defined area using your Quilting Goals Worksheet as a guide.

To keep my own design process carefree and easy, I work from the center outward filling four to eight shapes at a time.

The basics of the process can be broken down into three easy steps:

1. Isolate shapes.

2. Trace.

3. Fill.

Easy, right?

STEP 7: THE UNEXPECTED RESULTS

By working in small spaces without a complete, "perfect" road map to quilt, you'll be pleasantly surprised when you finish the quilt. It will be an unexpected moment of "Holy smokes! I made that!" mixed with "Oh, now *that* is really neat!"

Isolating Shapes

Choosing Marked Lines

One key element in practicing your quilting skills while using these linear designs is to recognize you absolutely do *not* need to use all the lines provided.

To help determine which lines to use, first decide your comfort level in quilting. Are you planning to focus on tight, meticulous designs, or would you rather have large designs? For the former, you may need a smaller, confined space; for the latter, a larger, open space.

Next, consider how much time you have for this project. Will this be an ongoing quilt project to work on each evening over a period of time, or a baby quilt that you need to finish by Saturday's shower? If you are in a hurry, choose larger shapes that are easier and faster to fill.

On the Quilting Goals Worksheet (page 39), use the linear design in the upper corner to plan your shapes. Use colored pencils or markers to shade in areas with similar fill designs.

Assign each color a fill style to use as a guide. For this design (Gingko, page 90), you might use:

Light blue: Pebbles • *Dark blue:* Ruler lines • *Yellow:* Open • *Light yellow:* Small swirls

Light green: Paisley teardrops • *Green:* Meandering • *Dark green:* Feathers

Perhaps for this design (Flora and Spike, page 84), you would make other fill selections, such as:

Light blue: Alternating grid design • *Dark blue:* Pebbles • *Light yellow:* Traditional feathers

Light green: Ruler lines • *Green:* Hooked feathers • *Dark green:* Small swirls (Echo each shape twice.)

Finally for this design (Solar System, page 108), these fills might work nicely:

Blue: Small feathers • *Dark blue:* Stacked swirls • *Light yellow:* Big pebbles

Light green: Meandering • *Green:* Parallel lines • *Dark green:* Paisley teardrops

Another way to isolate shapes is to cover the lines on the worksheet you don't want to use with white correction tape or fluid. This method also helps tremendously if you are overwhelmed by the number of lines.

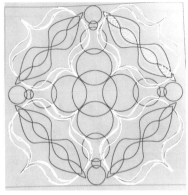

Helen Ernst's modified Grammar Nut design; the white lines represent where correction tape was used to simplify the design.

A third option is to draw over the lines you want to use with a marker to make them stand out.

ADDING LINES

Along with eliminating lines as you work, you may find the need to add lines or purposely connect design elements. Adding lines will depend on your personal style.

Original design

I chose to delete/ignore some lines, as shown in light blue.

To keep the design interesting, I added in additional design lines by connection points and shapes, as shown in pink.

Now that you have a loose road map—which you can always change at any time—go forth and stitch!

How to Use Marked Lines

Once the shapes are identified, or at least roughly planned in your mind's eye, vary how you will use each marked line.

For consistency in the options below, I chose to feature a cat's-eye shape and a feather-quilting fill to demonstrate how to vary line usage.

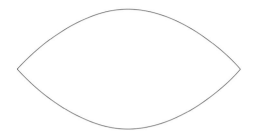

▷ Quilt along the marked line and use it to completely contain the fill design.

▷ Quilt along the marked line and use it as the spine (see Using Lines as Spines, page 37) to create the fill design on the outside of the shape.

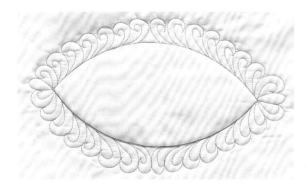

▷ Quilt along the marked line and use it as the spine to create the fill design within the shape.

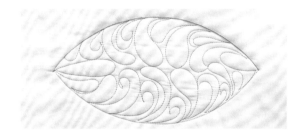

▷ Use the marked line as a guide to create a design with no spine along the path. This works for any type of fill that can cluster along a line, such as perfectly formed ruler-pebbles, random size pebbling, or other shapes.

▷ Use the marked line as a guide to suggest where the fill design should stop. It is quite amazing to see the shape defined without a hard, exterior line.

Juxtaposing shapes with organic-fill versus linear-fill designs really makes them stand out from one another. Give it a try!

Quilting Ideas and Goals

This chapter is intended to get the creative juices flowing. This is not a definitive list, but it does offer a great jumping-off point for machine quilting designs. The concepts presented here are areas that I personally focus on when working on these machine quilting skill builder projects.

Within each design presented, quilters will find their own level of expertise. Keep the variety of levels in mind: the design level varies based on each individual's skill level.

Consider manipulating a basic quilting motif to challenge yourself. For example, a popular traditional quilt fill is feathers, which can be broken into skill levels.

Beginner Work on the shape of each feather plume/petal. Make a feather design in a straight line.

Advanced Use feathers to completely fill negative space in a free-flowing design without determined lines and without any gaps in quilting coverage.

Aside from the quilting design motifs presented in this chapter, consider broader goals, as well. These concepts can be as easy as:

- Quilting faster or slower
- Switching thread colors
- Trying a different batting or thread
- Varying scale/size
- Working within defined spaces rather than edge-to-edge styles
- Balancing quilting density from shape to shape
- Varying soft organic lines mixed with rigid ruler work

Intermediate Manipulate the feather design into a shape or apply feathers to a predetermined curved line.

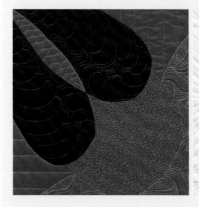

Using Rulers

Machine quilting rulers offer the opportunity for precise line-drawing designs. Both domestic sewing machines and longarm quilting machines can use rulers. Consult your sewing machine manual or dealer to equip the machine with a presser foot for free-motion quilting with rulers.

Free Motion Frame Quilting Feet Set (by Janome). I use the ¼" foot (*left*) with a convertible free-motion quilting foot holder (page 24, bottom left photo) on my domestic machine.

Note: *When using rulers with pieced quilts, they are often aligned with seamlines.*

Use the ruler by aligning it with a marked line. Keep in mind the presser foot is ¼" wide and will stitch ¼" from the ruler's edge. Rulers make alignment easy by providing a mark at each end of the straight line.

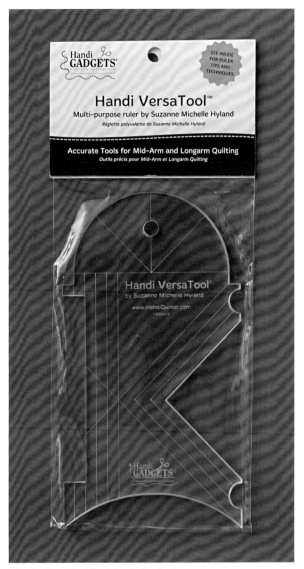

Handi VersaTool (by Handi Quilter)

The first step to create your machine skill builder design is to stitch on marked lines to define shapes. Not only is this good practice, but it makes for a very interesting quilt.

There are many other techniques you can practice with rulers.

ECHO QUILTING

This style of quilting is achieved when a quilting line is echoed an equal distance from an original quilting line. On most machine quilting rulers, echo lines are marked on the clear acrylic/plastic for exact line placement. Simply align the etched marked ruler line with the previously quilted line on the fabric, and quilt. It sounds easy, but like with everything, you will benefit from practice.

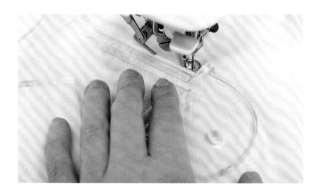

TRACING CURVES

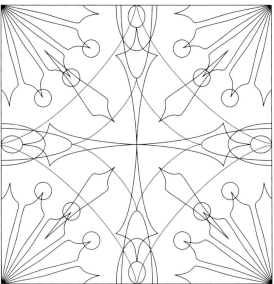

Tracing curves with a ruler is tricky. Of course, if the curve is the exact shape and size of a curved machine ruler, that helps tremendously. To build your skills, use a curved ruler to slide along the marked curve line to create a smooth quilted line. The ruler you work with will vary based on the tight or loose diameter of any specific curve.

For an advanced challenge, echo the curve!

SLIDING RULERS OVER LONG DISTANCES

Some quilters use channel locks on longarm machines to create continuous straight lines horizontally or vertically on the quilt. The channel lock secures the longarm wheels in either the X- or Y-axis directions. If this isn't an option for straight-line quilting, practice sliding the ruler along a marked straight line to stitch over long distances.

CURVED CROSS-HATCHING AND DIAGONAL GRIDS

 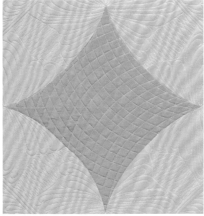 

These two ruler-based fills are quite similar, so we'll discuss them together.

Curved cross-hatching is a fill generally created using a curved ruler, whereas a diagonal grid is created using straight-line rulers. Diagonal grids may intersect at any angle (90° and 60° are the most popular).

1. Quilt an arched line.

2. Travel along the shape's edge to echo this arch using the ruler.

3. Keep the spacing between the lines the same. (For example, if the spacing between the lines is ½″, keep it ½″ for the next line.)

4. Continue in one direction until the space is filled. Clip and tie off the thread.

5. Create an arch in an opposing direction.

6. Travel along the shape's edge, then along the ruler to echo. Keep the same distance between the arched lines as in the original set of arches in Step 3.

7. Continue until the space is filled.

Note: *Make the design more advanced and challenging by varying the echo distance.*

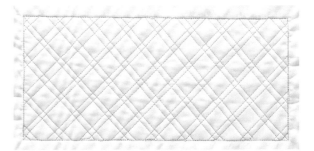

CIRCLES

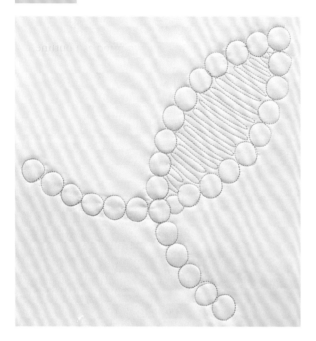

There are great rulers to help you stitch circles. I use the HQ Mini Circles Templates ruler (by Handi Quilter). To create a perfect string of circles, align the register mark with the marked line on the quilt.

When creating larger circles, the register marks on the ruler are invaluable. Align the etched register marks with crosshairs drawn on fabric.

The register marks also allow you to easily stack shapes in a consistent manner.

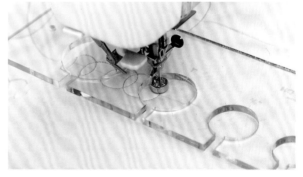

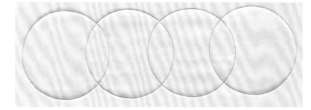

Note: *Make this design more complex by staggering the circle composition, creating concentric rings, using varying sizes, or filling the circle with traditional fill designs.*

Quilting Fills

Machine quilting fills are infinite and are only limited by your imagination. Keep that in mind as I outline a few popular fills that work great in the skill builder designs.

PEBBLES

Pebbles are a fantastic go-to to fill in space on nearly any quilt design. From traditional to modern, the pebble design fits all motifs.

Pebbles vary in size and precision.

Perfect circles (created using HQ Mini Circles Templates ruler)

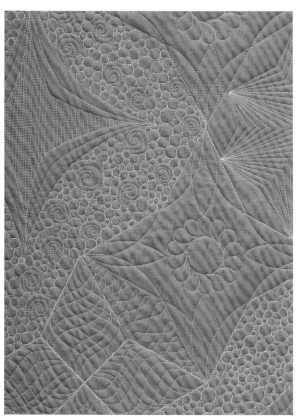

You may strive to create perfectly round circles stacked on each other, or you may want to practice mixing larger shapes with smaller ones. It's completely up to you!

1. Stitch a round figure eight.

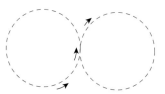

2. Backtrack one-quarter of the way around one circle.

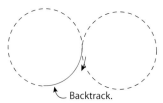

3. On the outside edge, start another circle. Backtrack around this shape one-quarter of the way so the needle is again on the outside of the nested shapes to add a fourth circle.

4. Continue adding circles by stitching a full circle and backtracking one-quarter of the way for each new circle added.

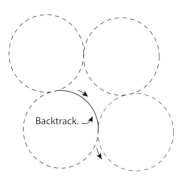

Note: *If you need the needle to travel to a different area of the quilt or a different edge of the shapes, simply trace over the circles until you reach the destination. Backtracking one-quarter of the circle is only a rule of thumb.*

STIPPLE, MEANDER, OR MICROSTIPPLE

Stippling and meandering are similar to pebbles in that they work on all types of quilts and are good go-to fills for all skill levels.

In many quilting discussions, this fill is referred to as both stippling and meandering. I like to differentiate; stippling features quilting lines much closer together (¼″ or less) while meandering can have the same fundamental design shape, but the quilting lines can be up to 2″ apart. In my mind, the main difference is that, with stippling, I cannot easily trace the stitching line with my finger or eye; in meandering, it is easy to follow the line once completed.

Create these designs in the same fashion. Simply make a wavy, organic line and make sure not to let the line cross over itself as you quilt.

Microstippling is an advanced design where the quilting stitches are so close together you cannot even trace the path with your eye or finger. Microstippling makes the quilt very flat and stiff and is often used to create colored shapes in quilt designs.

Meandering

Microstippling

Stippling

LINEWORK—WITHOUT A RULER

A few things you'll want to practice:

▸ Making lines parallel over longer areas without using a ruler

▸ Making "returns" trace the shape's edge, or making "returns" smooth curves

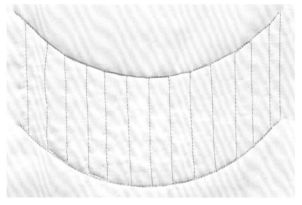

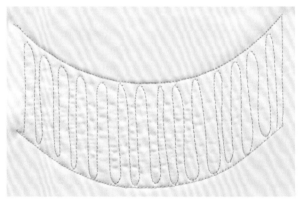

When filling smaller spaces, many quilters can make parallel-ish lines that flow back and forth from each edge. You guessed it, this design takes practice.

ALTERNATING GRIDS

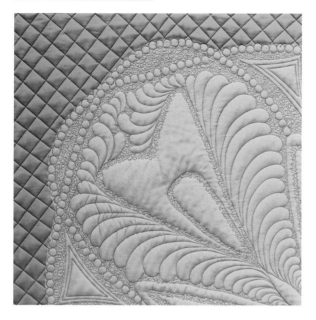

Tight linework is used to create alternating grids. The grids make areas of the quilt puff or recede into the background depending on the design placement.

Within a stitched shape on the skill builder, use a quilter's ruler and water-soluble marker to mark a grid. Grid squares can range from ½″ × ½″ to 3″ × 3″.

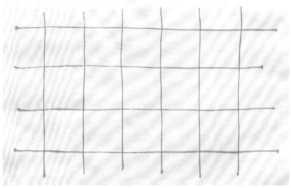

Consider quilting every other square in the grid, which creates a puff design.

Consider alternating the direction of linework to create a secondary visual design on the quilt.

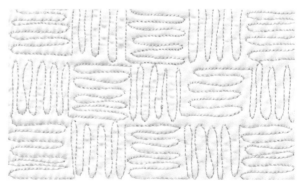

Perfect or elongated diamond shapes provide an opportunity to add more texture to the space. Notice how the fill differences between reasonably straight lines (below, top) and dense organic lines (below, bottom) create a unique feeling of structure or disorder within the design.

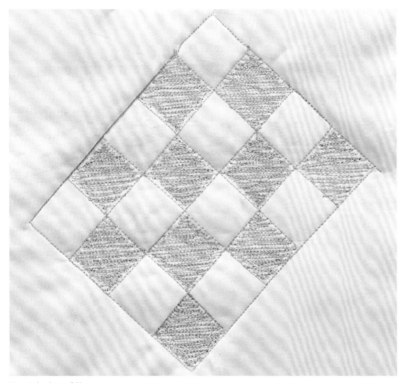

Straight-line fill

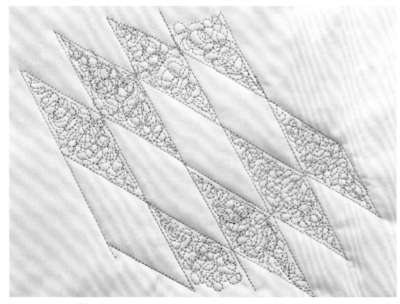

Dense organic fill

SWIRLS

Swirls can be created in a variety of ways. You might have a favorite method to create a swirl fill, but perhaps you have not tried the other styles. Now is the time!

I break swirls down into three categories: smooth, pointed, and stacked.

A **smooth swirl** continues in a single line without any hard points or corners.

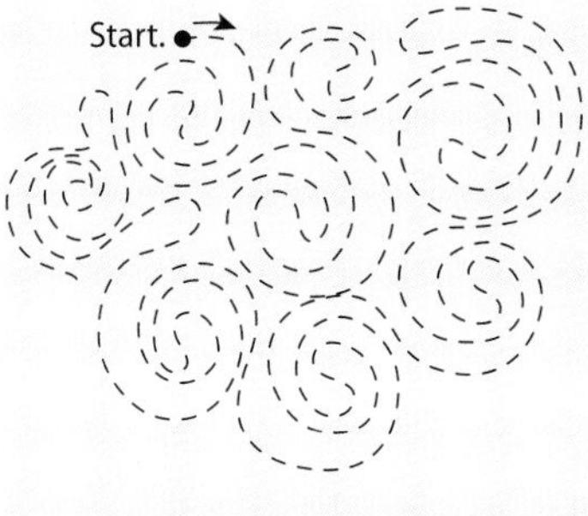

Pointed swirls add in points when echoing the swirl shape. These are particularly useful in camouflaging areas where the design may become trapped in the space.

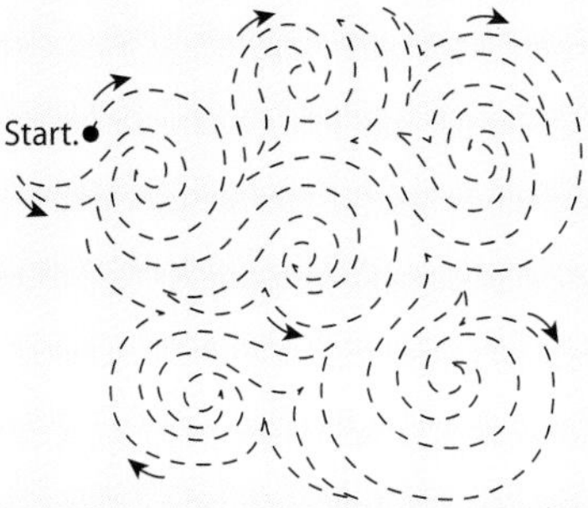

A **stacked swirl** allows swirl designs to crash into each other by tracing over the edge lines of previous swirl shapes.

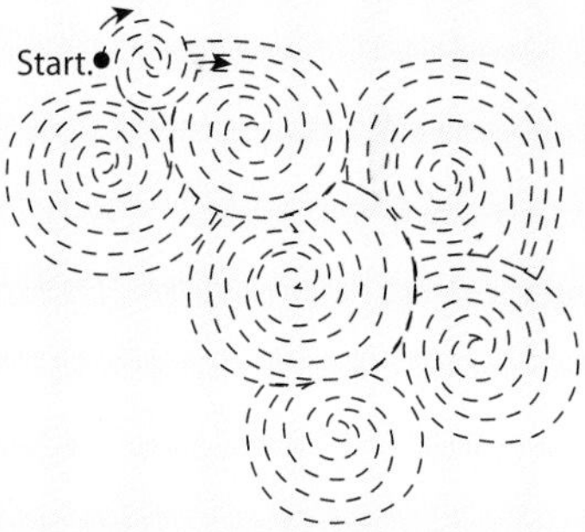

FEATHERS

Many quilting books focus entirely on feathers. This section isn't creating an entire book within a book; rather, it's providing guidelines for your next feather endeavor.

When creating a basic feather shape, make it as if you are drawing half of a heart.

To get started, ask yourself the following questions:

▶ Will the feather points rest on a center spine or line, or will they be free flowing?

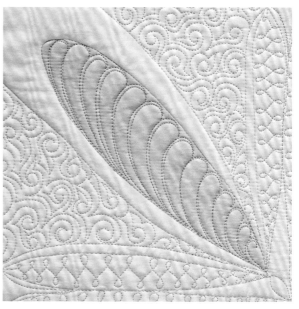

▸ Will the feathers follow along one edge or be a series of independent plumes and/or petals?

▸ Will the feather design fill the shape in a haphazard, whimsical fashion or will the feathers fill a defined shape completely but in an orderly fashion?

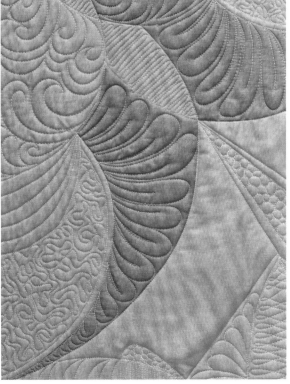

These design questions should get the wheels turning. Once you answer a question regarding the feathers, you'll find more questions follow. It really is like choosing your own adventure every time you tackle designs.

PAISLEY TEARDROPS

This design has many names. For fun, let's just pretend like it is universally called paisley teardrops. This design starts with a single teardrop shape, which is then echoed two or three times, meeting at the lower point.

The paisley teardrops can easily be scaled to fit a large or small space, and allow the thread to easily travel across the quilt.

Multiple designs can stem from this simple echoing process. Instead of making a teardrop, consider making a leaf or heart.

Many quilting design books include variations of the paisley teardrops design. Experiment and play!

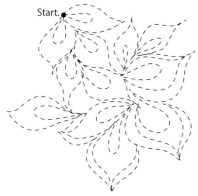

BOUNCING LETTER C'S

Using similar muscle memory as the paisley teardrops design, this is an excellent design to randomly cover a space or create a uniform design within a space. In both cases, an arched letter C is echoed from point to point along a shape's edge.

By varying the width of the echo and the tight curve of the C, this design can fill any space with interesting texture.

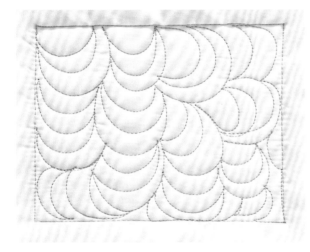

Creating the C's with an equidistant, consistent arch will create a uniform texture.

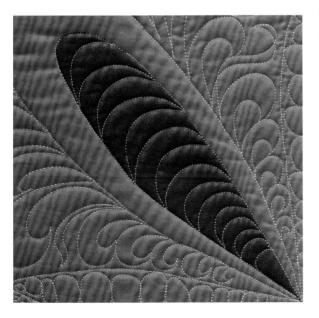

Using Lines as Spines

A large number of quilting designs are stitched along a planned line. In many cases, this planned line is referred to as a spine.

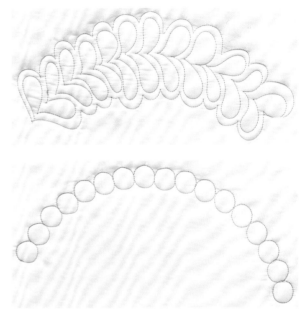

For your machine quilting skill builder projects, consider not only using the marked lines to define shapes, but using them also as spines to add spine-based motifs. *Remember:* The spine doesn't have to be a literal line. Use a line of circles or another shape as a spine to build your design. Endless possibilities.

Quilting Goals Worksheet

In Section 2: The Quilts (page 65), each design section contains a Quilting Goals Worksheet. On each worksheet, the overall design is provided in the upper right corner, with a space to the left to write your quilting goals. At the bottom, you can sketch quilting design motifs you are considering using as the fill designs within each shape of the overall design.

Not only will this worksheet help the quilting design stay on task, but it will serve as a reference while quilting. This is particularly useful to longarm quilters who may quilt a specific motif in the upper right and left corners, but may not remember exactly what the design looks like by the time the lower corners are ready to be quilted.

Quilting Goals Worksheets are available to copy from the book (see the list of pages below) or to download and print. For downloading instructions, see Downloading Designs and Worksheets (page 7).

WORKSHEETS YOU CAN COPY:

Blank worksheet   39

Circles   67

Concentric   73

Fascination Street   79

Flora and Spike   85

Ginkgo   91

Grammar Nut   97

Shark Attack   103

Solar System   109

The Grid   115

The Pinch   121

For examples of filled-out Quilting Goals Worksheets and their accompanying quilts, see the worksheet gallery (pages 40–54).

Quilting Goals Worksheet

Write Goals Here, such as "Feather within a Shape"
or "Quarter-Inch Echoes"

Practice Sketches

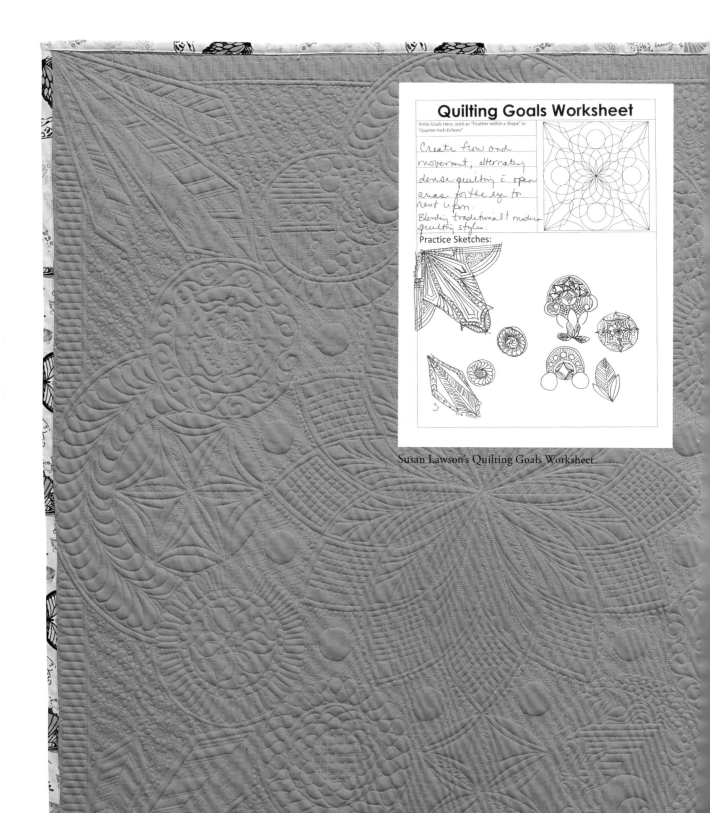

Quilting Goals Worksheet

Write Goals Here, such as "Feather within a Shape" or "Quarter Inch Echoes"

Create flow and
movement; alternating
dense quilting & open
areas for the eye to
rest upon.
Blending traditional & modern
quilting styles.

Practice Sketches:

Susan Lawson's Quilting Goals Worksheet

Quilting Goals Worksheet

Write Goals Here, such as "Feather within a Shape" or
"Quarter Inch Echoes"

Show off the circles around
the center shape ~ Make
the center a focal
design stand out with
filler

Practice Sketches:

Laura Pukstas's Quilting Goals Worksheet

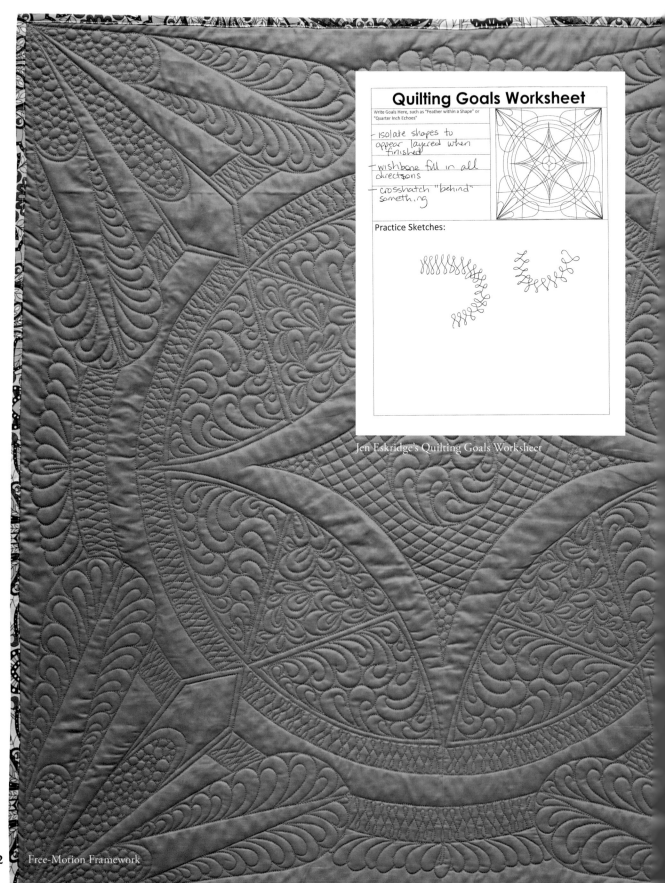

Quilting Goals Worksheet

Write Goals Here, such as "Feather within a Shape" or "Quarter Inch Echoes"

- Isolate shapes to appear layered when finished
- wishbone fill in all directions
- crosshatch "behind" something

Practice Sketches:

Jen Eskridge's Quilting Goals Worksheet

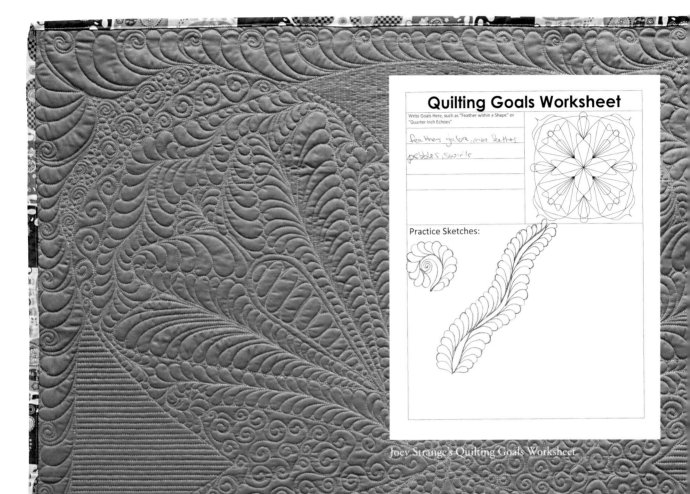

Quilting Goals Worksheet

Write Goals Here, such as "Feather within a Shape" or
"Quarter Inch Echoes"

feathers galore, more feathers
pebbles, swirls

Practice Sketches:

Joey Strange's Quilting Goals Worksheet

Quilting Goals Worksheet

Write Goals Here, such as "Feather within a Shape" or "Quarter Inch Echoes"

- slide ruler along straight line
- make pebbles in a pea pod
- stitch tight meander/stippling
- bump-back feathers
- random size hook feathers

Practice Sketches:

Jen Eskridge's Quilting Goals Worksheet

Quilting Goals Worksheet

Write Goals Here, such as "Feather within a Shape" or "Quarter Inch Echoes"

Fan clamshell fill

String of Pebbles surrounding shape

3/4" echo around shape

Rounded grid w/in curve

Practice Sketches:

Erin Monfort-Nelson's Quilting Goals Worksheet

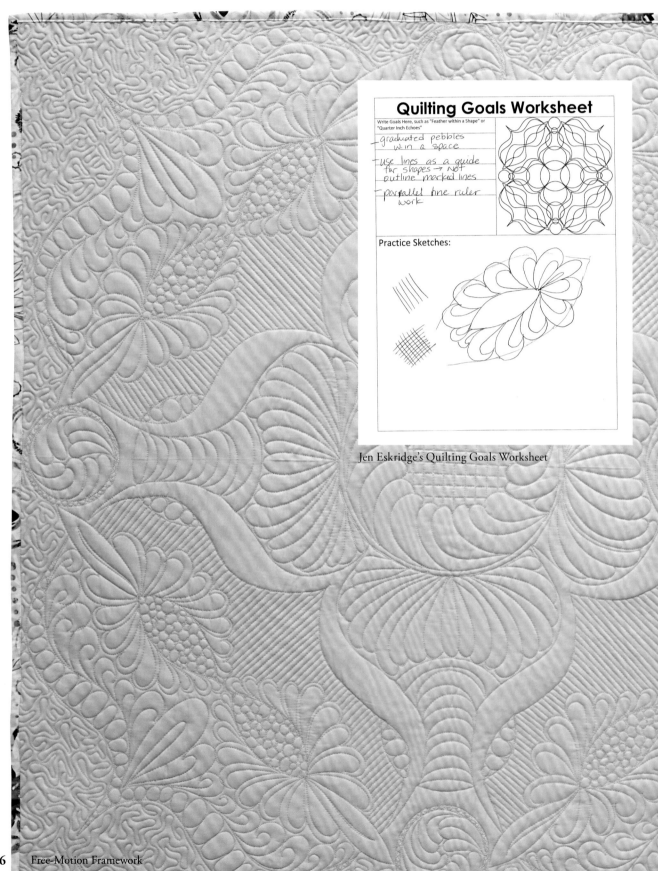

Quilting Goals Worksheet

Write Goals Here, such as "Feather within a Shape" or
"Quarter Inch Echoes"

- graduated pebbles
  w.in a space

- use lines as a guide
  for shapes → Not
  outline marked lines

- parallel line ruler
  work

Practice Sketches:

Jen Eskridge's Quilting Goals Worksheet

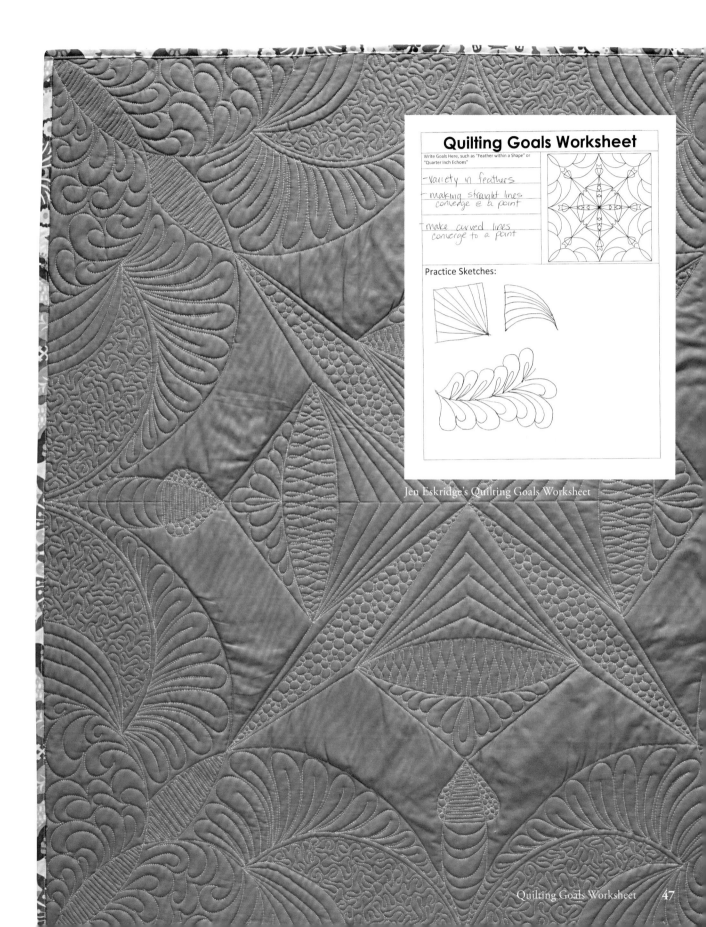

Quilting Goals Worksheet

Write Goals Here, such as "Feather within a Shape" or "Quarter Inch Echoes"

- Variety in feathers
- making straight lines converge @ a point
- make curved lines converge to a point

Practice Sketches:

Jen Eskridge's Quilting Goals Worksheet

Quilting Goals Worksheet

Write Goals Here, such as "Feather within a Shape" or
"Quarter Inch Echoes"

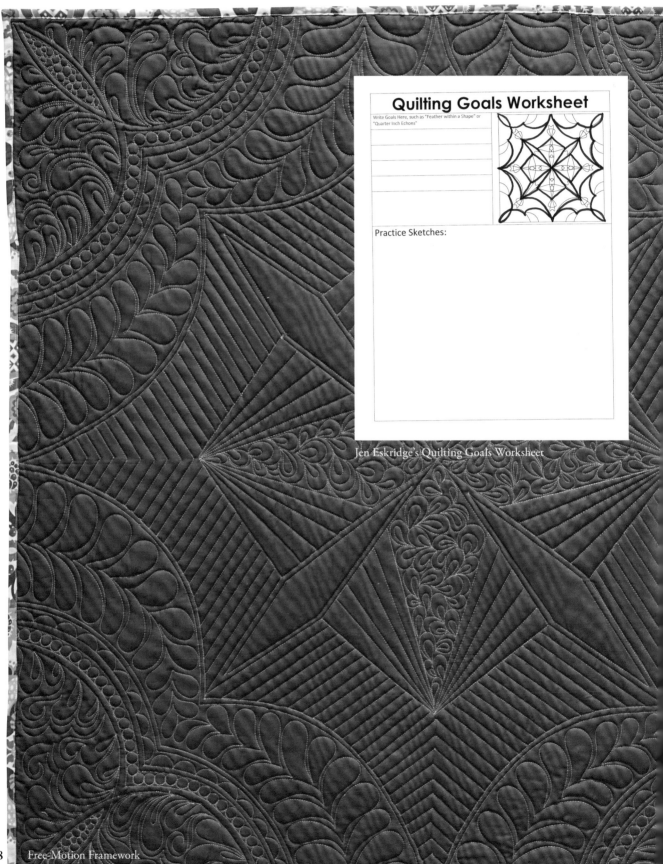

Practice Sketches:

Jen Eskridge's Quilting Goals Worksheet

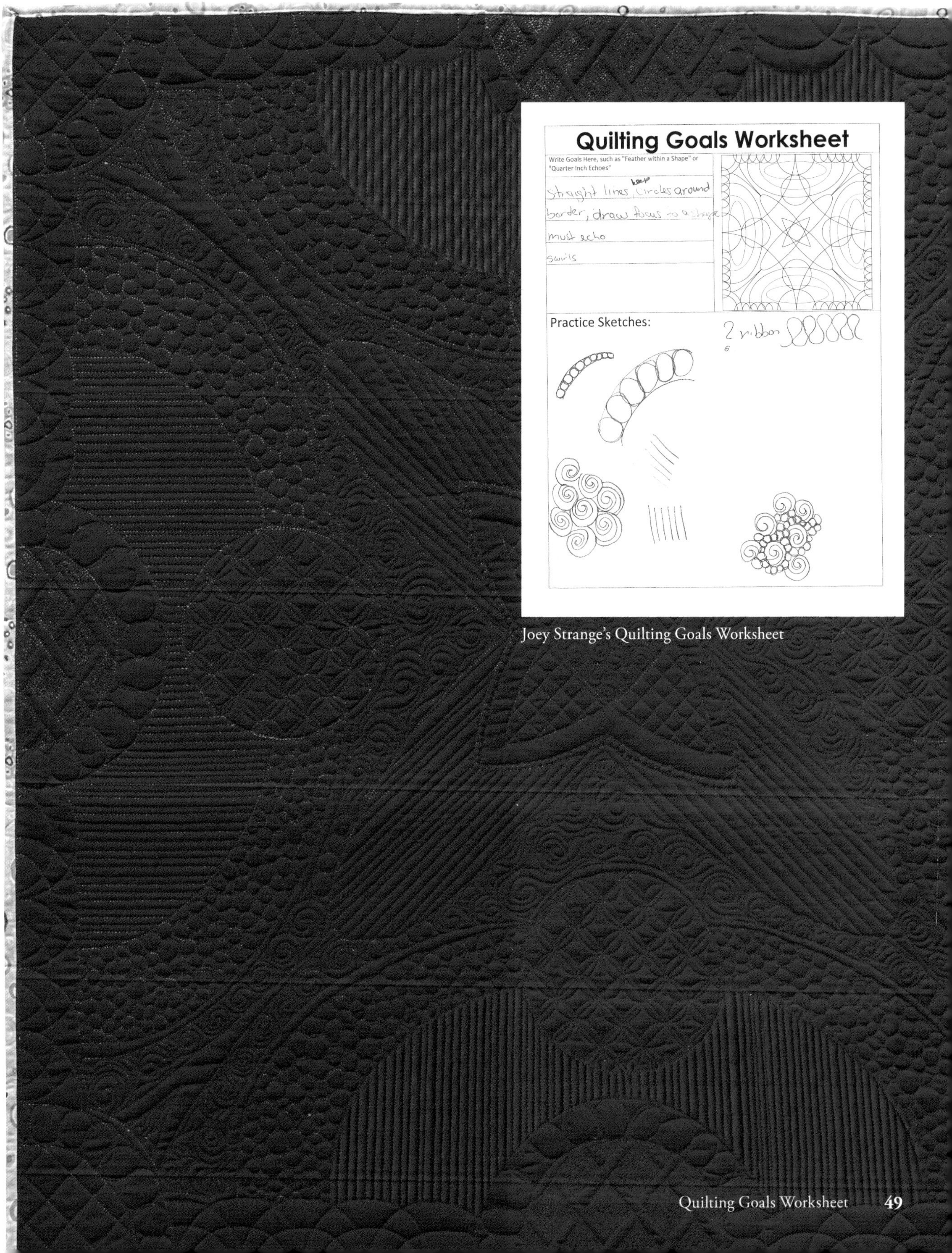

Quilting Goals Worksheet

Write Goals Here, such as "Feather within a Shape" or "Quarter Inch Echoes"

straight lines, circles around
border, draw focus to a shape
must echo
swirls

Practice Sketches:

2 ribbon

Joey Strange's Quilting Goals Worksheet

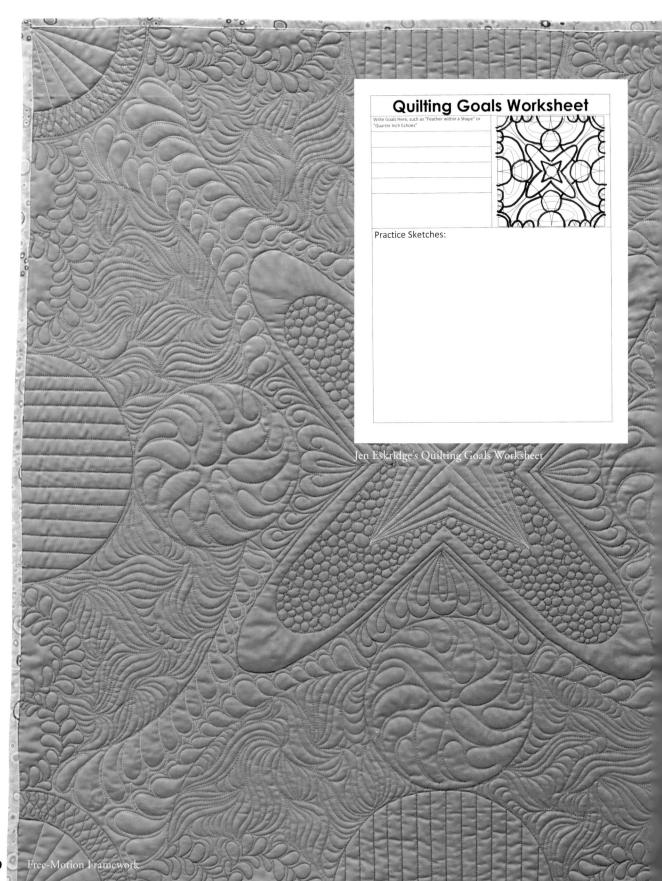

Quilting Goals Worksheet

Write Goals Here, such as "Feather within a Shape" or "Quarter Inch Echoes"

Practice Sketches:

Jen Eskridge's Quilting Goals Worksheet

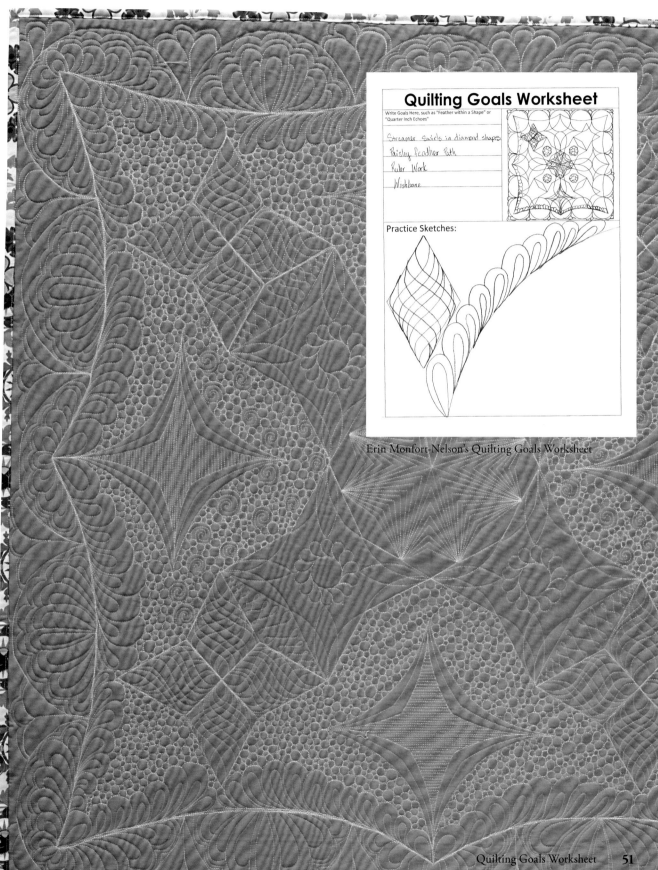

Quilting Goals Worksheet

Write Goals Here, such as "Feather within a Shape" or
"Quarter Inch Echoes"

Streamer Swirls in diamond shapes

Paisley Feather Path

Ruler Work

Wishbone

Practice Sketches:

Erin Monfort-Nelson's Quilting Goals Worksheet

Quilting Goals Worksheet

Write Goals Here, such as "Feather within a Shape" or
"Quarter Inch Echoes"

Create more of a traditional
motif using feathers and
some negative space

Practice Sketches:

Laura Pukstas's Quilting Goals Worksheet

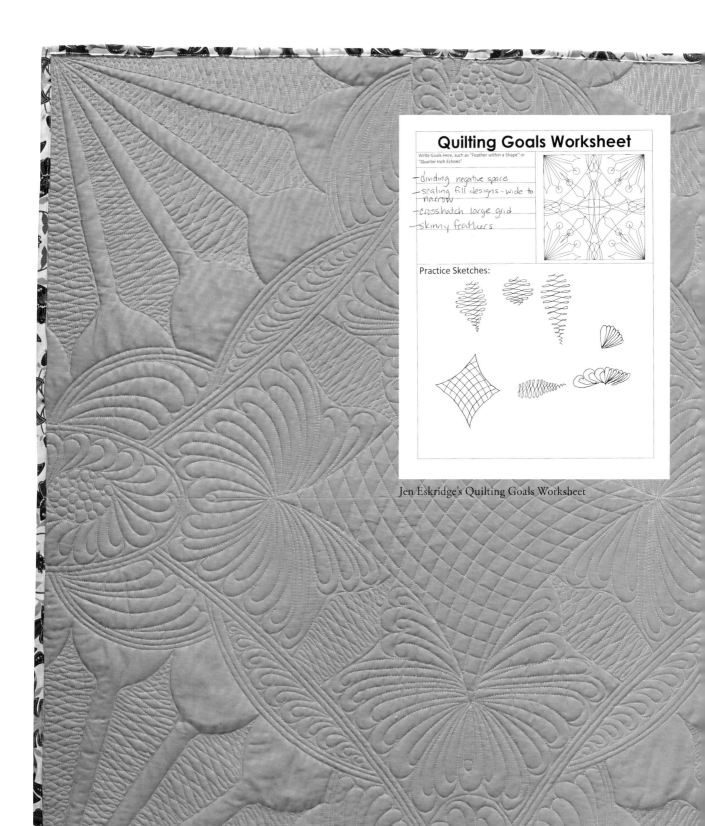

Quilting Goals Worksheet

Write Goals Here, such as "Feather within a Shape" or "Quarter Inch Echoes"

- dividing negative space
- scaling fill designs - wide to narrow
- crosshatch large grid
- skinny feathers

Practice Sketches:

Jen Eskridge's Quilting Goals Worksheet

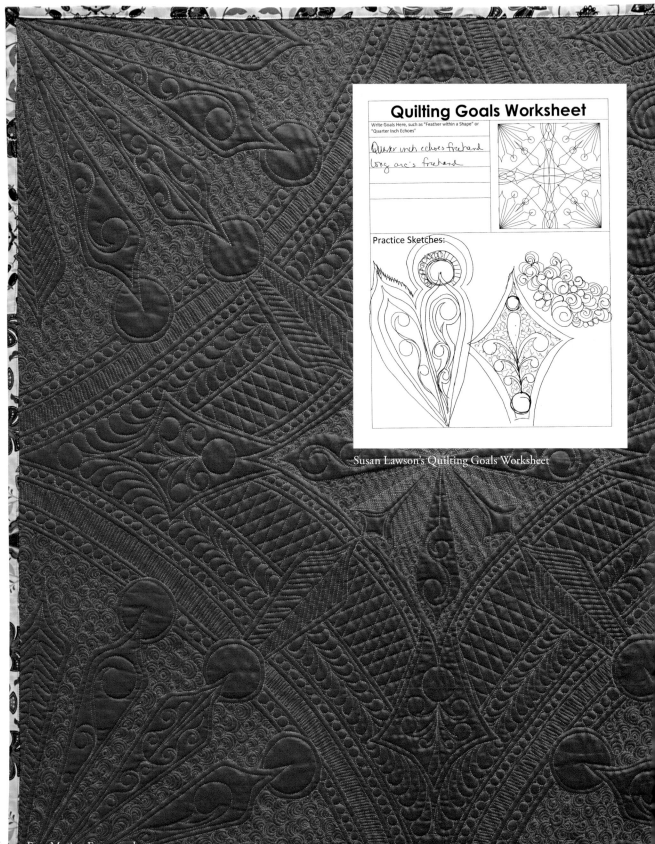

Quilting Goals Worksheet

Write Goals Here, such as "Feather within a Shape" or "Quarter Inch Echoes"

Quarter inch echoes freehand
long arc's freehand

Practice Sketches:

Susan Lawson's Quilting Goals Worksheet

Making Larger Quilts

You love the idea of a skill builder, but don't love the idea of a wallhanging. I totally understand! This chapter is for you!

There are a couple options to use the designs in this book to create larger quilts.

Borders

Borders can be added to any design. Here's how:

1. Trace the linear design to the focus/center fabric as described in Step 4: Print and Mark Design Lines (page 12).

2. Use a larger ruler and rotary cutting tools to trim the marked fabric 1″ past the marked lines.

3. Measure the square.

4. Add borders to the project—as many, and in any size, as you want. Consider adding pieced borders or solid borders to create interest.

 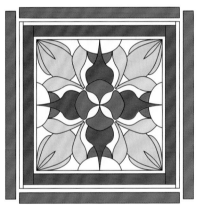

5. Quilt the center per your chosen design. Quilt the borders in a style in which you are comfortable.

Trim 1″ beyond stitched design.

Multiples

Making multiples creates larger size quilts. It is easier to mark 40″ × 40″ squares and join them together rather than marking a very large quilt top at once.

1. Mark 2 or 4 squares 40″ × 40″, depending on your desired size.

Notice the new central design created in the center of a four-quilt intersection.

2. Use a larger ruler and rotary cutting tools to trim the marked fabric 1″ past the marked lines.

3. Join the squares.

4. If you'd like an even larger quilt, add borders to the project.

5. Quilt each quadrant and add interesting quilting fills between the designs. If all the quadrants are the same color, the quilting fill between will camouflage any horizontal and vertical seamlines.

Use Linear Designs to Finish Traditional Quilts

The design concepts originally stemmed from the idea to make a wholecloth quilt without a cumbersome plan or design. In development, it became apparent these linear motifs may also be used to finish traditional quilts, which have 12″ or 15″ blocks. The steps that follow will show you how.

STEP 1: CHOOSE A DESIGN

1. Download the linear design (see Downloading Designs and Worksheets, page 7) to fit a 12″ × 12″ or 15″ × 15″ square. To print, determine which are the 8½″ × 11″ tiled pages you need and fill in the Page Range. Press Print.

2. Tape together the 4 sheets, matching the printed lines.

3. Trim to size.

12″ Circles design and 15″ Gingko design

STEP 2: CHOOSE LINES

Choose a line to stitch, not fill. You may opt to add a quilting fill inside the shapes, but it isn't necessary on this smaller scale.

Notice the lines print light gray. For smaller blocks, stitching all lines produces a very densely quilted project. If you prefer to use the lines as a guide, simply choose the lines on which to stitch and trace them with a permanent marker.

Dense quilting for smaller blocks

Medium quilting in a small block; gray lines omitted

Light quilting in a small block; more gray lines omitted

Like the larger
wholecloth designs,
you may opt to select
feature lines to quilt.
A different grouping
per block will create a
unified, coordinated
quilting design.

Central pods with floral elements added and
ellipses on each side

Central pods and corner design selected

Partial central pods, a different floral center,
and corner elements

The following line selections have been taken from the Gingko design (page 90).

STEP 3: TRANSFER TO QUILT

Use the tracing methods outlined in Step 5: Transfer Design Lines to Quilt (page 13) to transfer the desired lines to the quilt top.

STEP 4: QUILT

Layer the quilt sandwich. Quilt by hand, by domestic sewing machine (using a free-motion quilting foot or walking foot), or by longarm quilting machine.

 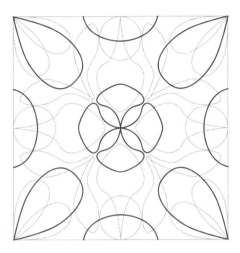

Central gingko flower with leaf and elliptic shapes in corners and on sides

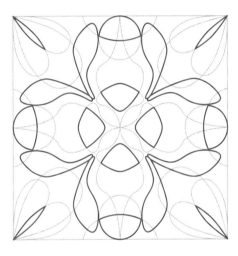

Pods and secondary shapes forming a central pattern with corner accents

 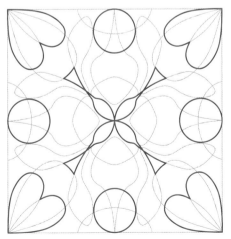

Hearts and circles surrounding a modified central motif

Thread and Batting

Considerations When Choosing Threads

This is not the end-all gospel to thread selection, simply the approach that works for me. You may find that you want the finished project to have a different look or feel than what another quilter may want. You may also find that your machine has different sensitivities and preferences when it comes to thread.

THICKNESS

Thread is assigned a number to distinguish its weight, which can range from 12-weight to 100-weight.

A smaller number denotes a heavier weight. In quilting, heavier/thicker threads tend to sit on top of the quilt top and be more prominent in the design. A thick thread may also make the quilt stiff if the quilting design motif is dense and very close together, such as microstippling (page 29).

A larger number denotes a lighter thread that will not be as noticeable on the surface of the quilt and will have a soft drape, or hand, once washed.

Typically, I like Glide 40-weight thread (by Fil-Tec). It's shimmery and gives just enough body to wash well and still show the time and effort invested in the quilting stitches.

FIBER CONTENT

Like fabric, thread is purchased by fiber content. Consider your quilt's end-use when selecting the thread. Popular thread fiber contents are cotton, polyester, silk, blends, and rayon. Depending on your machine, you may find that cotton threads make more lint, requiring the machine to be cleaned and oiled more often. Or you may find that a certain fiber content doesn't hold the right tension as it travels through your machine. For me, 100% polyester works great. For best results, consult your sewing machine manufacturer's suggestions or jump in with a trial-and-error process.

A WORLD OF COLOR

Each skill builder design creates a wholecloth quilt. Keeping that in mind, adding a layer of color to a simple blank canvas creates an incredible look. Choose a color palette you enjoy and plan shapes symmetrically. Changing thread colors will take a few minutes longer, but it's worth it when you see the depth in the design.

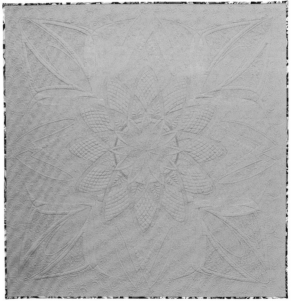

Batting

This is how I approach batting selection, but you'll find opinions will vary.

When making a 40″ × 40″ square quilt, approach batting selection with the project's end-use in mind.

If you're making a baby quilt or a quilt to be used and washed, consider Quilter's 80/20 cotton/polyester batting (by Fairfield) or 100% cotton batting. Both products will shrink slightly and will be soft and snuggly when used.

If you're making a wallhanging, consider using two layers of 100% cotton, or 100% needle-punched polyester batting. These allow the quilt to hang stiff while still providing a bit of puff in the quilting designs.

If you plan to fold and ship the quilt to a show or gift recipient, consider using wool batting, as it doesn't easily hold a crease.

Whichever batting you choose, note the suggested quilting density and care on the packaging.

Blocking

Blocking is the process of making the quilt lie square and flat after the project is finished. It is important, especially in densely quilted designs, because the quilt will start to waffle and shift as it is quilted. The blocking step is also useful for our purposes for a couple reasons:

▸ A 40″ × 40″ square quilt is a great wallhanging, and wallhangings look fantastic once they are squared up.

▸ We marked the entire quilt top. The submerge step in blocking will help remove any marking lines or ink residue.

How to Block a Quilt

1. Submerge the finished and bound quilt in a bathtub or large sink. If you are worried that the fabric colors may bleed, add a color dye-catcher.

2. Let it soak for 5–20 minutes.

3. Drain the water and gently wring out excess water from the quilt. If necessary, place the quilt in a washing machine's spin cycle to remove even more water.

4. Layer 3–5 towels on a carpeted floor. Carefully spread the quilt on top of the towels.

5. Measure the distance across the quilt in both directions along the top, middle, and bottom. If they are not the same, pull and press the quilt to encourage it to lie flat and equal. Notice the measurement may not be 40″ × 40″.

6. Along the top edge of the quilt, pin every 3″–6″ directly into the carpet, perpendicular to the floor.

7. Use a quilter's ruler to create a square corner. Place the ruler in the corner and pin along the side of the quilt every 3″–6″.

8. The corners should be square and the sides should be parallel to each another. If they are not, remove the pins and make a few adjustments.

9. Use a ceiling fan or a box fan to help dry the quilt.

Note: *As with any craft, there are many methods of blocking a quilt, from the method provided above to pinning to a design wall and/or foam insulation to spritzing the quilt top with a water bottle. Feel free to use this only as a jumping-off point and adapt the methods to best suit your needs.*

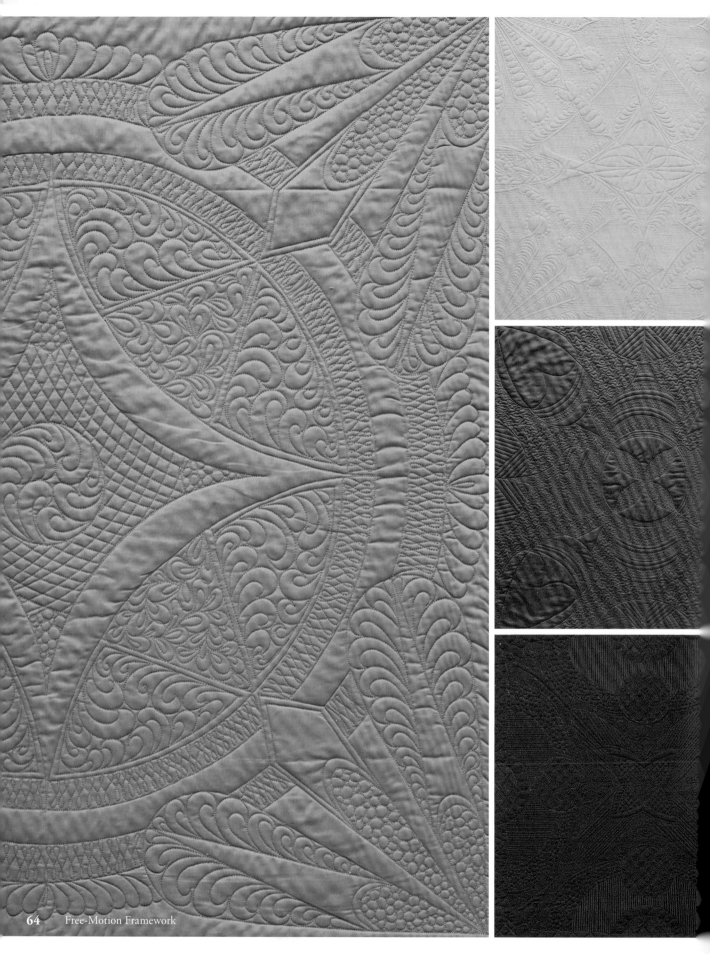

2

The Quilts

The following 40 quilts presented are grouped by linear design. Each design is interpreted by four different quilters. With a total of 17 quilters, you'll see quite a range of style. The free-motion and rulerwork quilting appears as unique as a person's handwriting in regards to their personal style. Remember, each quilt is created at the skill level of the quilter. All the designs are different and all represent challenge and growth.

Enjoy viewing the pieces side by side and take note of the linear outline per quilt. The quilters omitted or added lines as needed for their vision, following the "fill in simple shapes" process in Isolating Shapes (page 16). To help you visualize, you'll see a linear quadrant to note which lines were used from the original design.

For instructions on downloading the linear designs, see Downloading Designs and Worksheets (page 7).

You can do this!

Circles

Let's start with a simple shape: the circle. This design focuses on radiating shapes from the center. Some circles were pulled and squished while others were elongated and fattened. Personally, I created this linear design to develop more skills using circle rulers.

You'll see that two quilters, Susan Lawson (page 68) and Laura Pukstas (page 71), used circles to showcase a quilting-fill sampler design.

TIP Print this design's quadrant four times to ensure the center points line up when transferring the markings to the wholecloth.

QUADRANT

LINEAR DESIGN

Quilting Goals Worksheet

Write Goals Here, such as "Feather within a Shape"
or "Quarter-Inch Echoes"

_____

_____

_____

_____

_____

_____

Practice Sketches

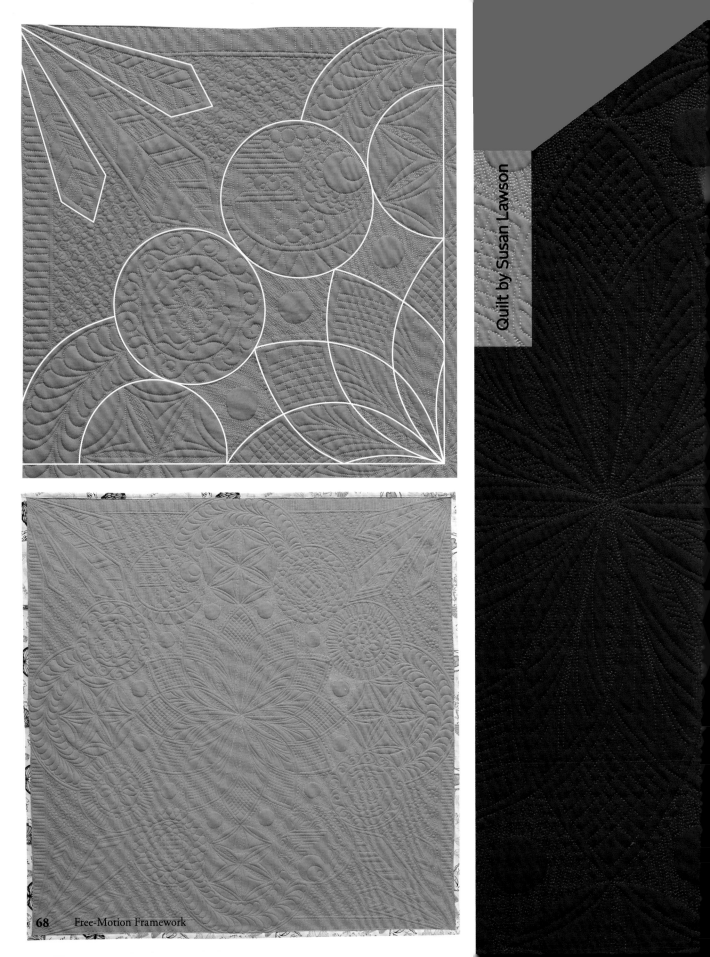

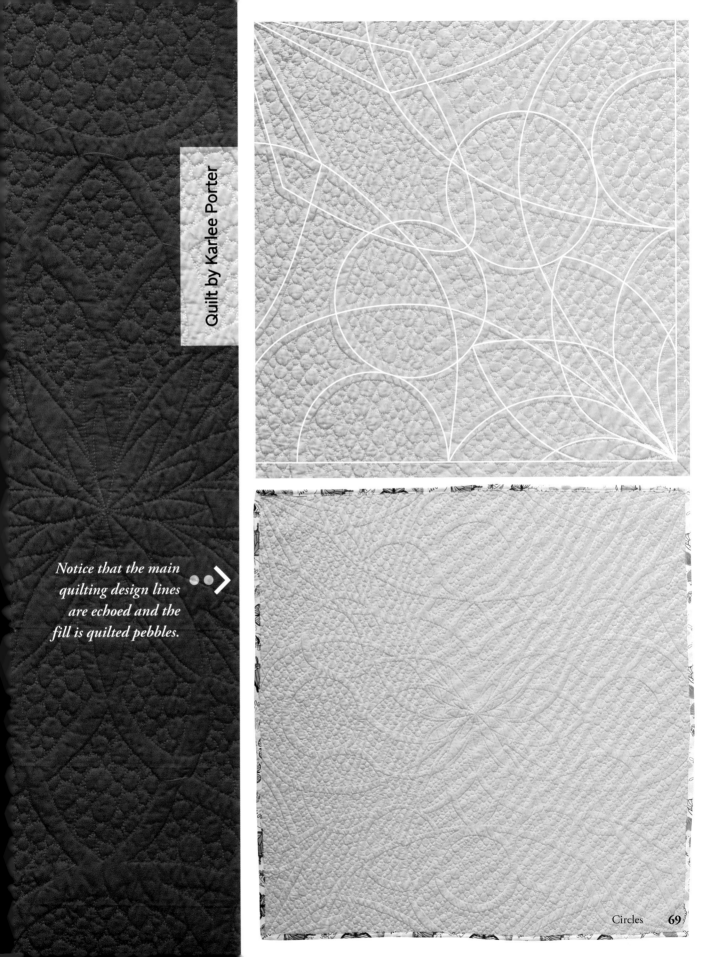

Notice that the main
quilting design lines
are echoed and the
fill is quilted pebbles.

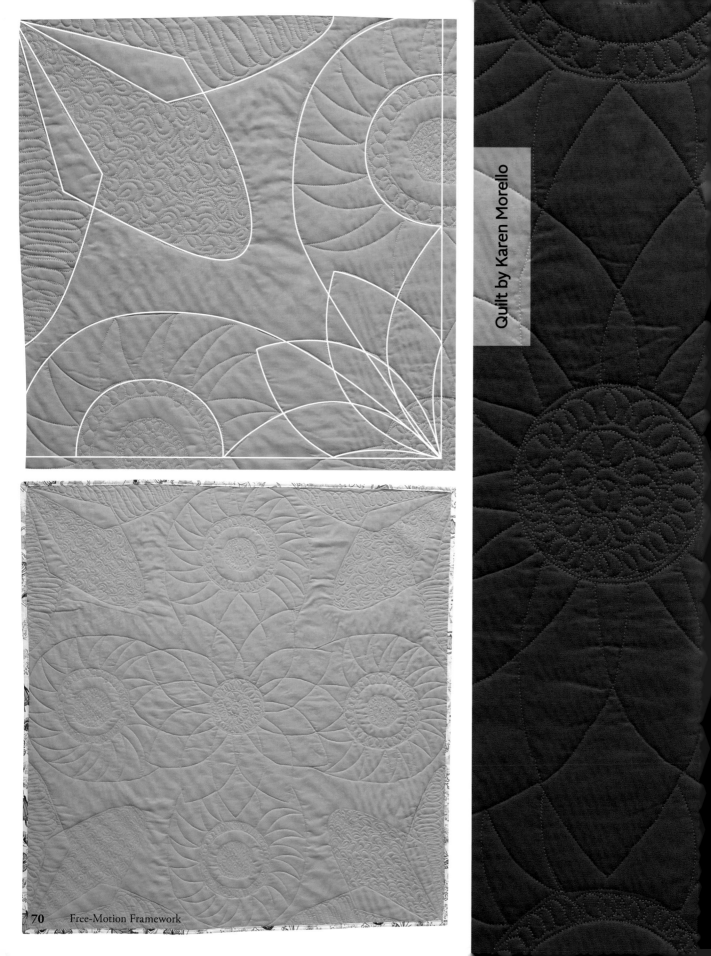

Quilt by Karen Morello

Concentric

This concentric design focuses on repeating shapes within each other. The idea is to trace the concentric lines consistently with a ruler, while still working on isolating and filling shapes. The nesting designs created interesting overlap spaces, which yielded totally unique quilts.

QUADRANT

LINEAR DESIGN

Quilting Goals Worksheet

Write Goals Here, such as "Feather within a Shape" or "Quarter-Inch Echoes"

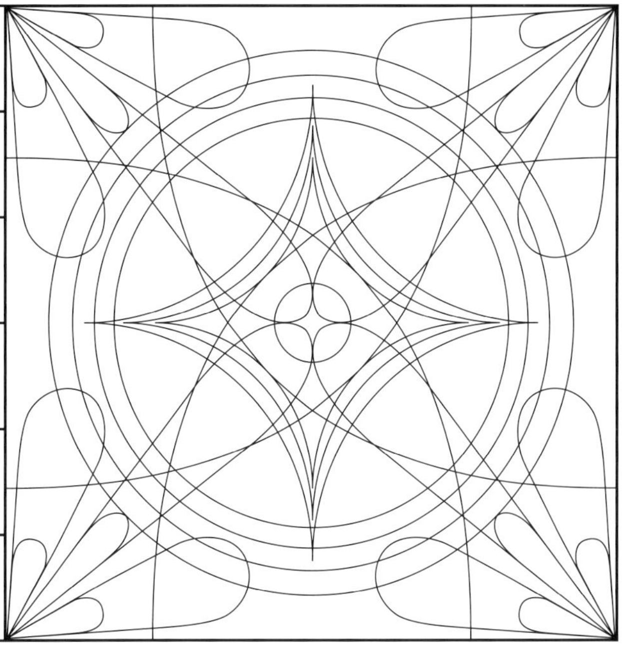

Practice Sketches

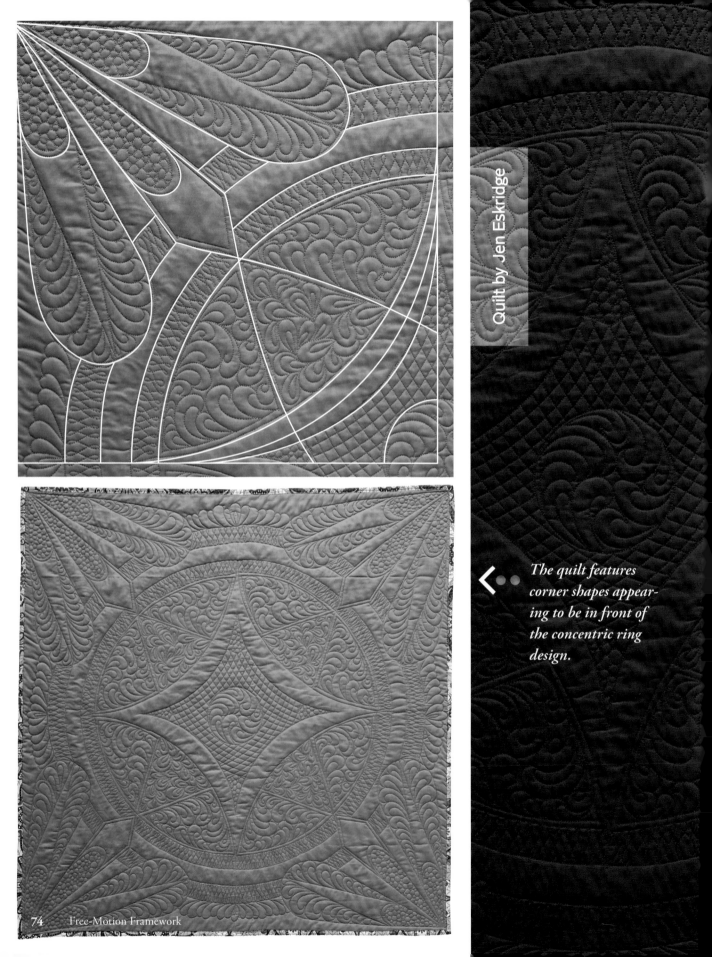

Quilt by Jen Eskridge

The quilt features corner shapes appearing to be in front of the concentric ring design.

Quilt by Marion McClellan

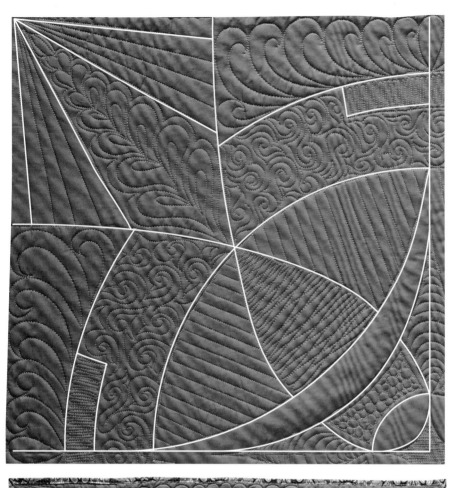

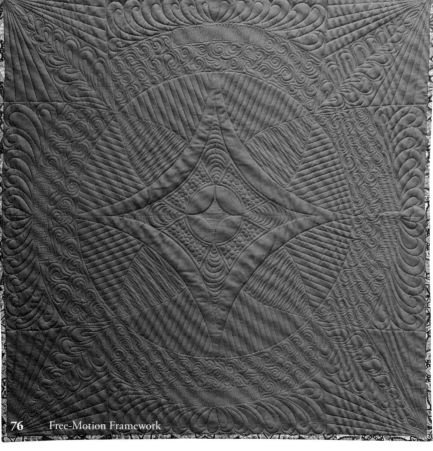

Notice how Sterling used minimal lines to practice quilting fills while still creating an interesting, densely quilted design.

Fascination Street

Aptly named, this design is based on the first linear design I created to begin my journey down the wholecloth and skill-building road. This design led to my fascination with the endless ways in which a design may be manipulated while retaining its cohesive composition.

QUADRANT

LINEAR DESIGN

Quilting Goals Worksheet

Write Goals Here, such as "Feather within a Shape"
or "Quarter-Inch Echoes"

_____

_____

_____

_____

_____

Practice Sketches

Quilt by Melanie Leckey

Jo completed this whole design on a domestic home sewing machine.

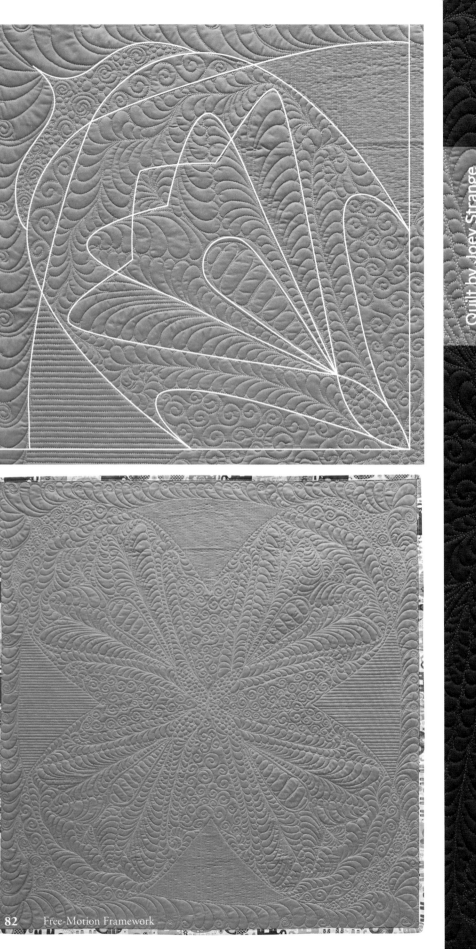

Free-Motion Framework

Quilt by Joey Strange

Quilt by Helen Ernst

Notice Helen's use of pebbles to define larger shapes. She created her quilt on a domestic sewing machine.

Tracing the quadrant design and the marked edge of the quilt makes it easier to plan a quilting design to the project's edge. The traced line will be a quilting boundary and a trim line once you are done quilting.

Flora and Spike

The Flora and Spike design features long points, ideal for using a straight ruler. To compliment the hard-edged spikes, the design also features a softer, floral element. The design points are quite tight at the center of the design. Beginners may want to omit those points to showcase an allover design at the center, as I did in my dark purple quilt (page 87).

QUADRANT

LINEAR DESIGN

Quilting Goals Worksheet

Write Goals Here, such as "Feather within a Shape"
or "Quarter-Inch Echoes"

_____

_____

_____

_____

_____

Practice Sketches

Free-Motion Framework

Quilt by Joanna Marsh

Flora and Spike   **87**

Geraldine created her quilt on a domestic home sewing machine.

Quilt by Colleen Eskridge

Flora and Spike   **89**

Ginkgo

Inspired by the ginkgo leaf, gentle curves, and circles, this design radiates from the center. When creating the design, hearts accidently appeared in the corners, but as you'll see in a couple of quilts, the hearts are a comfortable, familiar shape in which to fill.

Quilters commented that a few of their shapes looked like tennis rackets or holiday ornaments. Add those to the surprise hearts and you'll never know what design will emerge.

QUADRANT

LINEAR DESIGN

Quilting Goals Worksheet

Write Goals Here, such as "Feather within a Shape"
or "Quarter-Inch Echoes"

Practice Sketches

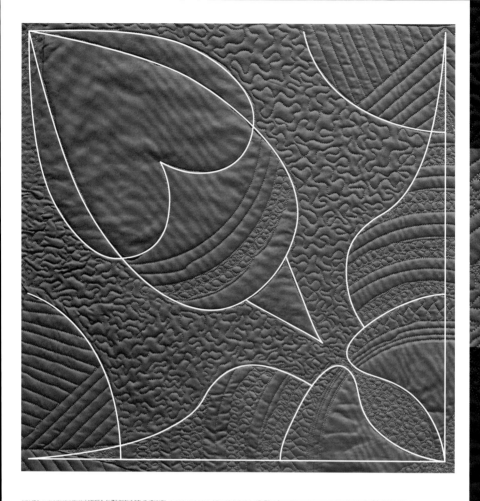

Quilt by Karen Morello

Quilt by Teresa Silva

Notice the greatly simplified design lines.

Quilt by Shannon Schlosser

Quilt by Erin Momfort-Nelson

Grammar Nut

This design started with four simple sets of curly brackets. Can you see one pair in each corner? A simple superhero mask shape was added within the pair, and a composition started to reveal itself.

Look at the four Grammar Nut quilts and note the difference in background fill designs. Diagonal rulerwork, meandering, swirls, and clean negative space gives you an idea of the many options you can use on your own design.

QUADRANT

LINEAR DESIGN

Quilting Goals Worksheet

Write Goals Here, such as "Feather within a Shape" or "Quarter-Inch Echoes"

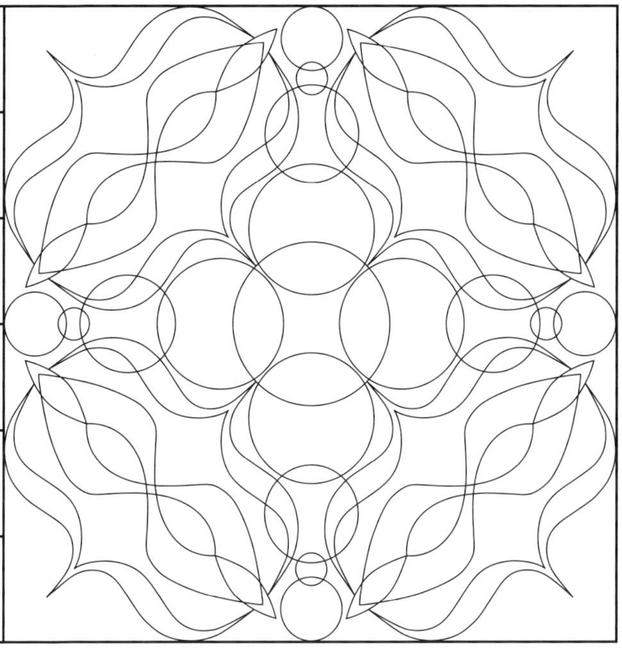

Practice Sketches

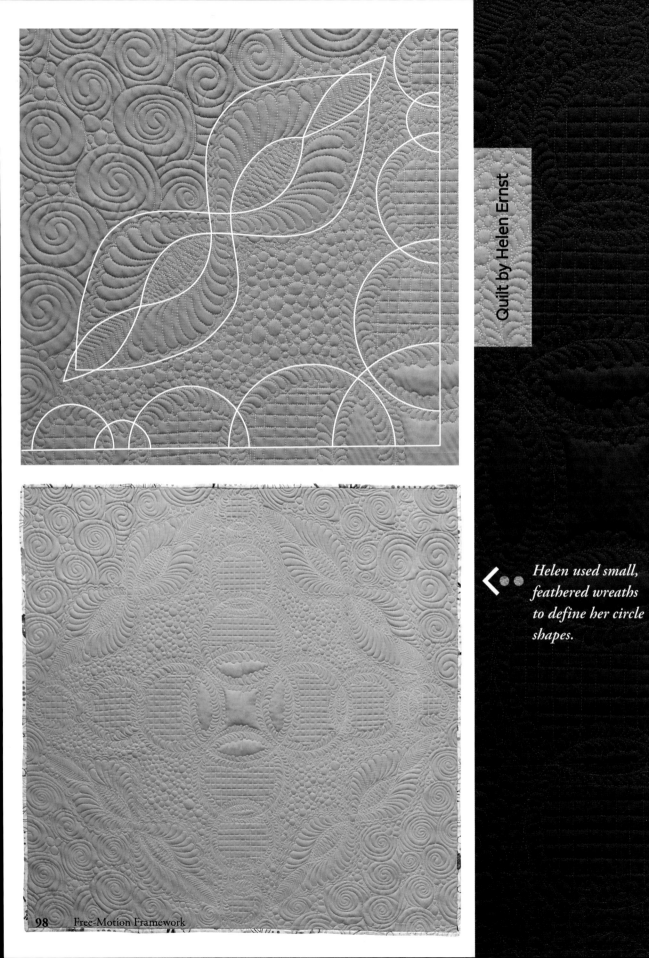

Helen used small, feathered wreaths to define her circle shapes.

Quilt by Jo Oliver

Notice how Jo used only one edge of each curly bracket shape to create a much larger, interesting design in each corner.

Quilt by Jen Eskridge

In this quilt, I did not trace the superhero mask area of each quadrant, but rather used it as a loose guide or bounding box for the feather motif.

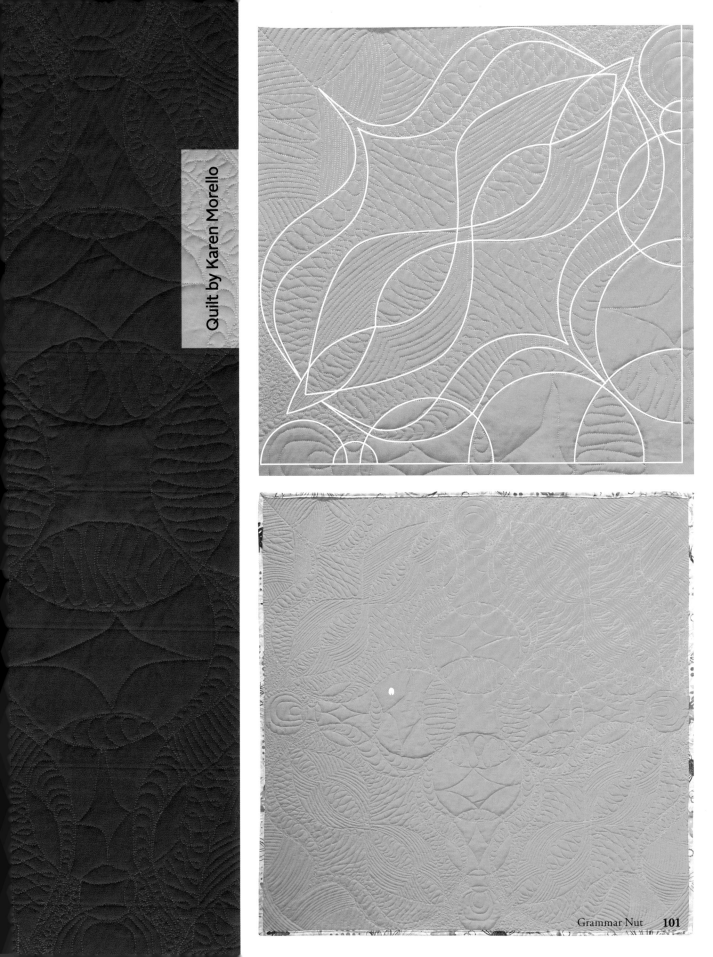

Quilt by Karen Morello

Shark Attack

Quite a quirky name for a quilt design! The pointed arches along the perimeter of the design reminded me of that infamous shark fin and, thus, Shark Attack was born. The mix of smooth curves and pointed intersections allows for ample quilting ideas.

From no-quilting to dense quilting, you can achieve amazing effects!

QUADRANT

LINEAR DESIGN

Quilting Goals Worksheet

Write Goals Here, such as "Feather within a Shape"
or "Quarter-Inch Echoes"

Practice Sketches

Notice how my quilt has shapes unquilted, which appears to make them "puff" from the design. Using wool or high-loft batting will increase this effect.

Joanna traced over her shape lines with many passes, creating a unique, modern outline in her design.

 Using minimal original lines and contrasting gold thread, this design offered me the opportunity to study ruler work and converging-line designs.

In Geraldine's quilt, notice how the four densely quilted triangles cause the quilt to actually appear as though the fabric is white in that area.

Solar System

As I manipulated and elongated shapes, such as turning circles into ovals, I couldn't help but notice the design started to orbit! Once that took shape, I added a few more planet-esque circles, creating the Solar System composition.

QUADRANT

LINEAR DESIGN

Quilting Goals Worksheet

Write Goals Here, such as "Feather within a Shape"
or "Quarter-Inch Echoes"

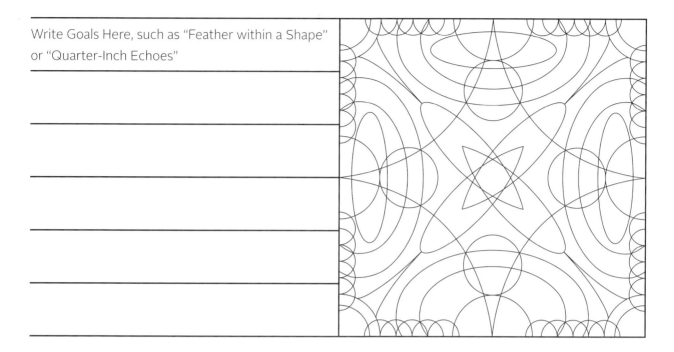

Practice Sketches

Quilt by Marion McClellan

Quilt by Joey Strange

Quilt by Jen Eskridge

Three thread colors are featured in this quilt, using color as an additional element of depth in the overall composition.

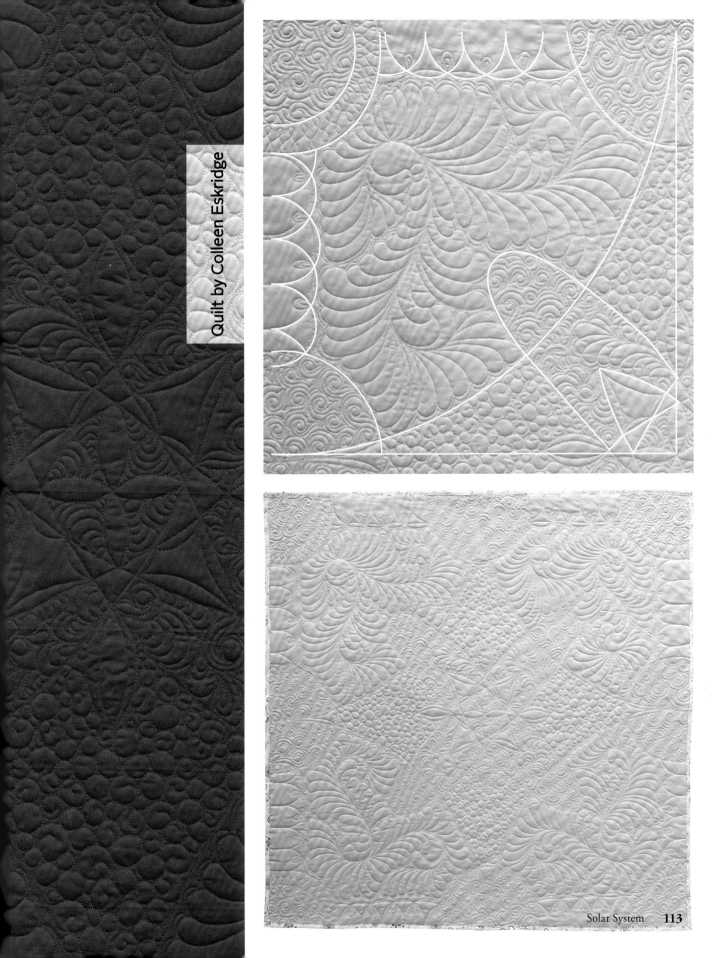

The Grid

This is the only design in the book that was created using a grid rather than a radial concept. It is so interesting to see the quilters' interpretations of the design, as it still appears to converge at the center.

QUADRANT

LINEAR DESIGN

Quilting Goals Worksheet

Write Goals Here, such as "Feather within a Shape"
or "Quarter-Inch Echoes"

Practice Sketches

The center feathers appear to float in front of the pinch-star motifs.

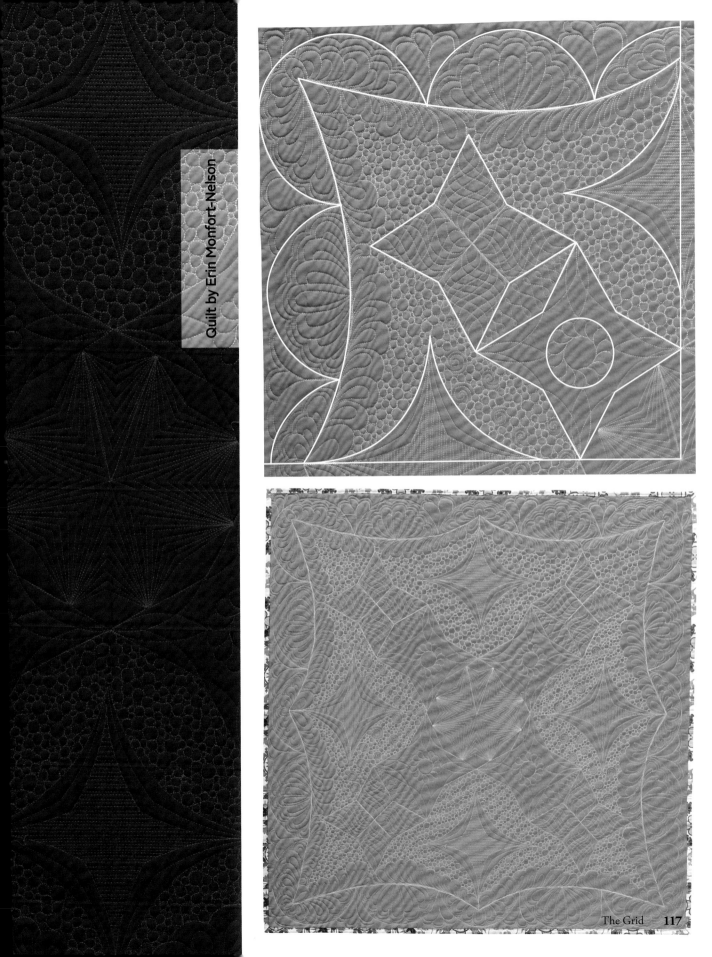

Quilt by Laura Pukstas

The outer perimeter of the quadrant is traced so the feathers have a bounding box and the quilter has a trim guideline.

By echoing around the outside of a defined shape, you can increase its visual size. See the difference in the relative star sizes in Teresa's quilt.

The Pinch

Start with a simple oval. Pinch one side. Pinch the other side. Stretch the oval.

This is the basic method I used to create this composition. It was a personal challenge to try to include the maximum number of pinched oval variations to create a unique and balanced design.

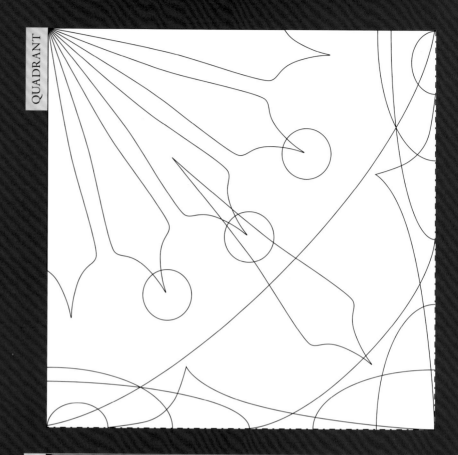

QUADRANT

LINEAR DESIGN

Quilting Goals Worksheet

Write Goals Here, such as "Feather within a Shape"
or "Quarter-Inch Echoes"

_____

_____

_____

_____

_____

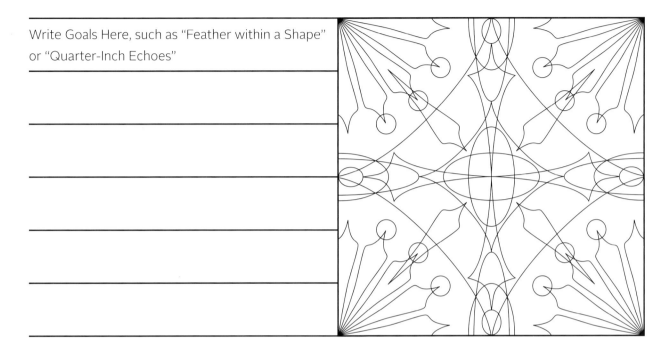

Practice Sketches

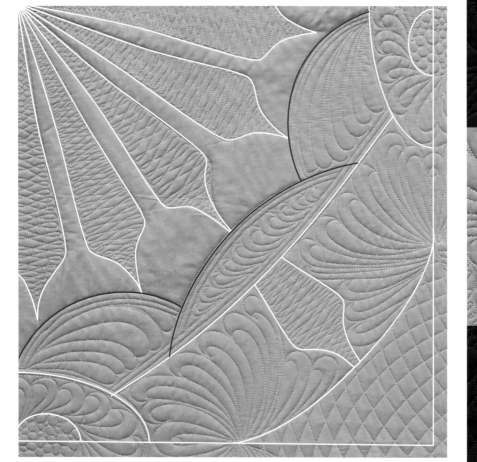

During the quilting phase—not the marking or tracing phase—I added lines to the design to make the negative space more interesting in this quilt. Remember, the provided design is your practice design and you can add or subtract anything you like!

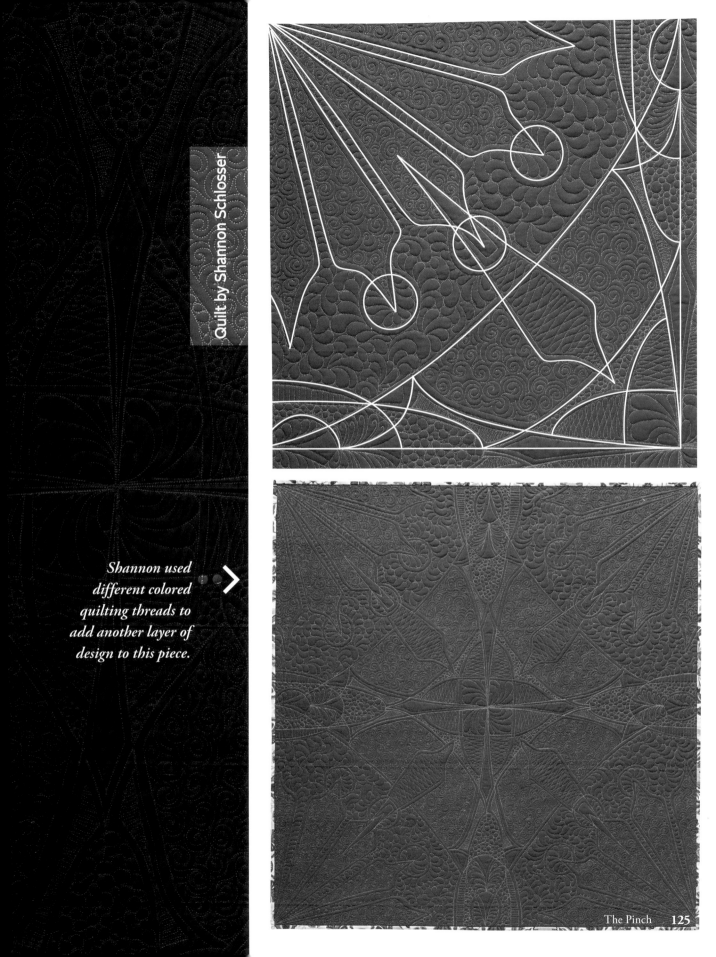

Shannon used different colored quilting threads to add another layer of design to this piece.

Contributing Quilters

Helen Ernst
Helen Ernst Longarm Quilting

Website: helenernstlongarmquilting.com

Instagram: @tillwequiltagain

Colleen Eskridge

Instagram: @colleeneskridge

Sterling LaBosky
Sterling Quilt Company

Website: sterlingquiltcompany.etsy.com

Instagram: @sterlingquiltco

Susan Lawson
Seamingly Slawson Quilts

Website: seaminglyslawsonquilts.
blogspot.com

Instagram: @slawsonquilts

Melanie Leckey
Oh Sew Loved

Website: ohsewlovedquilting.com

Instagram: @ohsewloved

Joanna Marsh
Kustom Kwilts and Designs

Website: kustomkwilter.com

Instagram: @kustomkwilts

Marion McClellan
My Quilt Diet

Website: myquiltdiet.blogspot.com

Instagram: @myquiltdiet

Erin Monfort-Nelson
Ad Astra Quilting

Website: adastraquilting.com

Instagram: @ad_astra_quilting

Karen Morello
boom*N*grannie's quilting

Website: boomngranniequilting.com

Jo Oliver

Instagram: @joliver326

Karlee Porter
Karlee Porter Design

Website: karleeporter.com

Instagram: @karleeporterdesign

Laura Pukstas
Stitch In Time Quilts

Instagram: @stitchintimequilts

Shannon Schlosser
Sew You Like It

Website: sewyoulikeit.etsy.com

Instagram: @shanschlosser

Teresa Silva
Quilting Is My Bliss

Website: quiltingismybliss.com

Instagram: @quiltingismybliss

Joey Strange
Joey's Quilting Co.

Website: joeysquiltingco.com

Instagram: @joeysquiltingco

Geraldine A. Wilkins
Living Water Quilter

Website: livingwaterquilter.com

Instagram: @livingwaterquilter

About the Author

Jen started sewing in 1993 on a tan Singer sewing machine. Her mother taught the basics, and Jen made her first quilt that very same year. She didn't use any books or templates, and that poor quilt eventually fell apart—though it was recycled into a curtain and duct taped over a dorm room window.

Fast forward a bit: Jen earned a bachelor of science in apparel design from Louisiana State University in 1998. By 2003, she found herself quilting and sewing for her own company, ReannaLily Designs. During that time, Jen also taught quilting at a national crafting store. The website was launched in 2007.

Jen is based near San Antonio, Texas, and when not writing or designing, she travels to share her trunk show, lecture, and teach quilting/sewing to shops, guilds, and groups.

Jen is the author of four books: *Deploy That Fabric*, *Learn to Sew Easy Curves*, *Hexagons Made Easy*, and *The Quilted Clamshell*. Jen's designs have been featured in multi-author books, as well as more than 20 magazines.

VISIT JEN ONLINE!

Email: reannalilydesigns@gmail.com

Website: reannalilydesigns.com
(Be sure to check out Jen's longarm quilting services and her best-selling seam guide, too!)

Instagram: @reannalilydesigns_jen

ALSO BY JEN ESKRIDGE:

Want even more creative content?

Make it, snap it, share it *using* #ctpublishing